7/97

D1175346

A Dark Night's Dreaming

UNDERSTANDING CONTEMPORARY AMERICAN LITERATURE
Matthew J. Bruccoli, General Editor

Volumes on

Edward Albee • John Barth • Donald Barthelme • The Beats
The Black Mountain Poets • Robert Bly • Raymond Carver
Chicano Literature • Contemporary American Drama
Contemporary American Horror Fiction
Contemporary American Science Fiction
James Dickey • E. L. Doctorow • John Gardner
George Garrett • John Hawkes • Joseph Heller
John Irving • Randall Jarrell • William Kennedy
Ursula K. Le Guin • Denise Levertov • Bernard Malamud
Carson McCullers • Toni Morrison
Vladimir Nabokov • Joyce Carol Oates
Tim O'Brien • Flannery O'Connor • Cynthia Ozick
Walker Percy • Katherine Anne Porter • Thomas Pynchon
Theodore Roethke • Philip Roth • Mary Lee Settle
Isaac Bashevis Singer • Gary Snyder • William Stafford
Anne Tyler • Kurt Vonnegut • Tennessee Williams

A Dark Night's Dreaming

Contemporary American Horror Fiction

Edited by

Tony Magistrale
Michael A. Morrison

University of South Carolina Press

© 1996 by the University of South Carolina

Published in Columbia, South Carolina, by the
University of South Carolina Press

Library of Congress Cataloging-in-Publication Data

A dark night's dreaming : contemporary American horror fiction/
    edited by Tony Magistrale, Michael A. Morrison.
        p.   cm. — (Understanding contemporary American literature)
    Includes bibliographical references and index.
    ISBN 1–57003–070–7
    1. Horror tales, American—History and criticism.   I. Magistrale,
Tony.   II. Morrison, Michael A., 1949–   .   III. Series.
PS374.H67D37   1996
813′.0873809—dc20   95-40646

Manufactured in the United States of America

99 98 97 96   4 3 2 1

To my wife Mary,
who has steadfastly encouraged my interest in horror fiction, and to my
colleagues and friends in the departments of English and Physics and
Astronomy at the University of Oklahoma, who helped me make it part
of my professional life.

—Michael A. Morrison

This book is also dedicated to Jennifer Magistrale, Jane and Randy
Amis, Sherry Brown, and to Polly Binns—for putting up with me
through the years.

—Tony Magistrale

Contents

General Editor's Preface

The volumes of *Understanding Contemporary American Literature* have been planned as guides or companions for students as well as good non-academic readers. The editor and publisher perceive a need for these volumes because much of the influential contemporary literature makes special demands. Uninitiated readers encounter difficulty in approaching works that depart from the traditional forms and techniques of prose and poetry. Literature relies on conventions, but the conventions keep evolving; new writers form their own conventions—which in time may become familiar. Put simply, *UCAL* provides instruction in how to read certain contemporary writers—identifying and explicating their material, themes, use of language, point of view, structures, symbolism, and responses to experience.

The word *understanding* in the series title was deliberately chosen. Many willing readers lack an adequate understanding of how contemporary literature works; that is, what the author is attempting to express and the means by which it is conveyed. Although the criticism and analysis in the series have been aimed at a level of general accessibility, these introductory volumes are meant to be applied in conjunction with the works they cover. They do not provide a substitute for the works and authors they introduce, but rather prepare the reader for more profitable literary experiences.

M. J. B.

Preface

The Design of This Book

In this volume, critics of literature, film, and popular culture intro-
duce the themes, preoccupations, and major works of contemporary
American horror fiction. The core of this book features essays on the
lives and narratives of six writers who have dramatically shaped contemporary American horror fiction since the early 1970s: Tony Magistrale on
Thomas Harris, Edwin F. Casebeer on Stephen King, Lynda Haas and
Robert Haas on Anne Rice, Bernadette Lynn Bosky on Peter Straub,
Douglas E. Winter on William Peter Blatty, and Mary Pharr on Whitley
Streiber. Each essayist highlights primary themes and images in the ma-
jor works of his or her subject writer and further links these concerns to
the ongoing tradition of modern American horror.

Framing this core section are two wide-ranging essays that define a
broad context for reading American horror fiction, in general, and the
canons of these six writers, in particular. Michael A. Morrison begins
with a survey of major developments in the field since 1980 (the publication date of Stephen King's historical analysis *Danse Macabre*). Following
the individual author essays, Michael J. Collins examines the complex
interaction between American horror fiction and American horror film.
Collins shows that the confluences of these two mediums is an essential
feature of contemporary Gothicism crucial to the understanding of both
fiction and film. Those readers seeking recommendations for further
reading and commentary on the genre will find more information in the
bibliography. The work of the novelists and film directors featured in
this volume, with the notable exception of Stephen King, has received
very little serious interpretative criticism. It is unfortunate that for some
readers there exists a gap between popular writers and "serious" or "acceptable" ones. In part, this book is dedicated to narrowing that gap.

The editors wish to acknowledge the International Association on
the Fantastic in the Arts (IAFA), which unknowingly midwifed this
book. This project was conceived at one IAFA conference, contributions

were solicited from the remarkable array of talented critics who attended another, and drafts of individual chapters were presented at a third conference. If the IAFA sometimes looks askance at horror fiction and those who read and write about it, the association continues to provide fertile loam for its serious study, and for that we are immeasurably grateful.

A Dark Night's Dreaming

Introduction

Tony Magistrale and Michael A. Morrison

Horror has figured prominently on the American literary scene since Charles Brockden Brown deftly appropriated the conventions and devices of the late-eighteenth-century British Gothic to peculiarly American ends in *Wieland* (1789). During subsequent decades, writers such as Edgar Allan Poe, Herman Melville, Nathaniel Hawthorne, William Faulkner, Nathaniel West, and Flannery O'Connor adapted the conventions of the British Gothic to narrate uniquely American preoccupations with sin and innocence, grotesquerie and obsession, and death and renewal.

The physical trappings of the eighteenth-century English Gothic novel—the unnatural biology of walls, staircases, tunnels, corridors, and enclosed spaces where psychosexually obsessed hero-villains pursued chaste maidens—gradually evolved into an American fiction that emphasized psychological terror over physiological fear. The haunted British bedchamber, in other words, gave way to the haunted American psyche; the subterranean fascination with perverse games of sexual intrigue and hysterical flight in Horace Walpole's *Castle of Otranto* (1764) attained a more profound intensity in the psychopathology of Poe's interior monologues.

Along with the pervasive influence of Puritanism, the Gothic remains one of the most important and consistent strains connecting the diverse elements of the American literary tradition. Nearly thirty years ago, Leslie Fiedler recognized, in *Love and Death in the American Novel*, that American literature has always been "bewilderingly and embarrassingly, a gothic fiction, non-realistic and negative, sadistic and melodramatic—a literature of darkness and the grotesque . . . a litera-

1

ture of horror."[1] While it is possible to trace the presence of the Gothic in contemporary mainstream American writers as different as Toni Morrison and Norman Mailer, horror fiction as a genre has been relegated largely to the margins of traditional academic scholarship. The genre's importance to American culture, however, is undeniable. Its inimitable influence on film, music, literature, fashion, theater, and the other visual arts continues to merit serious critical attention. From its inception as a harbinger of British romanticism through its diverse incarnations in two centuries of refinement and experimentation, the Gothic has continually recreated itself as artists have used it to reveal, magnify, and analyze the darkest impulses of human beings and their societies.

Contexts for Understanding Horror

During the decade of the 1970s, sociologist Christopher Lasch published *Haven in a Heartless World* and *The Culture of Narcissism*. In these books he argued that contemporary American society has lost its commitment to shared values and moral purposefulness. The diminished status of American institutions of authority—school, church, government, and the family itself—left in its wake a culture of individuals living in self-enclosed vacuums (a society of profoundly alienated narcissists). Lasch's books supply the statistical and theoretical basis for properly understanding some of the major issues at the heart of contemporary American horror.

Much of what occurs in horror art is symbolic; that is, its deepest meanings exist on a subtextual level. Beneath its veneers of tormented maidens, madmen, monsters, and the other archetypes of the genre, horror consistently reminds us of human vulnerability. Americans spend vast amounts of money and spiritual energy insulating themselves against the random intrusiveness of violence and perceived forces of social anarchy. Yet all around us our cocoons of self-preservation and denial show signs of stress and breakage: subway riders on their way home are murdered by strangers, young men are assaulted and killed for straying into the wrong neighborhood, women are raped in toilet stalls, children are pushed from rooftops for candy bars and designer sneakers.

Some people escape from the imminent reality of such horrors by denying their existence and by clinging to a perpetual suspension of disbelief. Horror art, on the other hand, prefers to see the reality flushed out into the open. As the ancient authors of tragedy understood most profoundly, the very act of watching our collective and personal fears reworked into a narrative affords the audience some measure of understanding and, perhaps, control over such experience. Thus, horror inspires a repulsion-attraction reaction in even its most ardent admirers: we are repulsed by images that are meant to threaten our security, yet simultaneously attracted to the drama and meaning of what they reveal. At its most significant level of meaning, the art of terror is concerned with detailing the tragic consequences of social and personal disintegration—it is the essential aesthetic medium for our time. This fact alone helps, in part, to explain the genre's enormous popularity. To be understood properly, the best horror fiction must be viewed as contemporary social satire that reveals—and often critiques—the collective cultural fears and personal anxieties of everyday life.

Horror art centers on forces of destruction—the domain of bedlam. Yet the tale of terror is not an exclusive exercise in loss and negation. Like any other genre, horror fiction reveals the complexities of what it means to be human, even as it often relies upon core definitions of otherness and exclusion. In *Danse Macabre*, Stephen King argues that the horror tale is an exercise in survival, that the audience is provided with an opportunity to gain profound insights into its fears and, by extension, to acquire an array of coping skills. For King, horror art is essentially a moral medium: it teaches us behavior to avoid, illustrates survival mechanisms worthy of emulation, and extols the virtues inherent in experiencing personal tragedy without being overwhelmed by it.

King would have us understand that classical tragedy and horror art are related. If a story has been aesthetically successful, the audience is stunned by how swiftly and ruthlessly the gods affect mortal life. In addition, both horror and tragedy rely upon phenomena Aristotle first recognized: that pity and fear inspire an audience and that in the stimulation of these emotions the possibility for reintegration, or catharsis, is born.

Here is the final truth of horror: It does not love death, as some have suggested; it loves life. It does not celebrate deformity but by dwelling on deformity, it sings of health and energy. By showing us the miseries of the damned, it helps us to rediscover the smaller (but never petty) joys of our own lives. It is the barber's leeches of the psyche, drawing not bad blood but anxiety. . . . We make up horrors to help us cope with the real ones. With the endless inventiveness of humankind, we grasp the very elements which are so divisive and destructive and try to turn them into tools—to dismantle themselves.[2]

The Monster and Its Audience

A distinguishing trait of horror art is the existence of a being that emerges to disrupt the personal and social relationships of the status quo. The horror monster sometimes embodies the worst aspects of these social and personal contexts (as does the creature in Stephen King's *It*), and always represents something threatening. As Noël Carroll argues, "when monsters cease to be threatening, they cease to be horrifying."[3] Regardless of its shape, the horror monster violates the norms and values of the society it attacks. Robin Wood has insisted that this assault be viewed as a force of political liberation, that horror highlights the oppressive elements of a culture through the emergence of a creature that "even in its overt nihilism offers the possibility of radical change and rebuilding."[4] In its evolution, the monster both embodies and manifests the fears and anxieties of its age. These sociopolitical concerns are exemplified in the specific types of transformations which occur in the horror tale. The civilized human gives way to the wolf, the educated man to the violent murderer, and the urbane psychiatrist to the cannibal. In each case, the monster represents some aspect of a repressed self transformed into the Other. This inherent duality often reflects the dichotomy of human nature: our faith in an ever-evolving civilized self that is shadowed by the lingering presence of sin and atavism.

As an audience, we greet the horror monster with a mixture of repulsion and secret identification. While part of us is appalled by its excesses and outrages, another part gleefully identifies with its rebellion against social, sexual, and moral codes. It is no surprise, for example, that the most engaging character in Thomas Harris's fiction remains Hannibal Lecter; or that Jack Nicholson's portrayal of Jack Torrance in Stanley Kubrick's adaptation of *The Shining* is still the most compelling figure in all the films that have been made of Stephen King's fiction. True to the Gothic hero-villains who preceded them—such as Lewis's Ambrosio, Beckford's Vathek, Melville's Ahab, and Stevenson's Jekyll/Hyde— Lecter and Torrance are perverse mixtures of goodness aborted and greatness twisted. The horror monster is seldom wholly unsympathetic; the reader is always aware of the Gothic villain's tortured mind and soul, and of the potential that is thwarted in his or her loss of moral balance.

Perhaps this genre's emphasis upon divided selves explains in part why the traditional audience for horror has always included a large teenage representation: by experiencing great hormonal changes and questioning authority and identity, teenagers seem to identify with the admixture of terror and liberation associated with a monster's physical transformation, assertiveness, and social rebellion. From this orientation, it is possible to argue (as James Twitchell does in *Dreadful Pleasures*) that the Gothic novel presents figures that threaten society's established concepts and categories. The art of horror sometimes forces us to examine that which we have repressed in ourselves and in our culture—the secret impulses toward selfish behavior, sexism, and racism, for example. When these elements surface symbolically in the form of the monster, they undercut our collective effort to see ourselves as good men and women living in a free and decent democracy.

If it is possible to read horror as a force that subverts and challenges hegemonic culture by revealing its secret urges and anxieties, then there is at least as strong a need to interpret the genre's insistence that the monster be destroyed as an essentially conservative reaction. The horror story attempts to overcome the monster either through the inclusion of some superhuman event or through the power of the victim to outwit or survive the creature. Once the monster has been vanquished, the horror narrative achieves closure and the audience breathes easily once again. The audience is now secure in the knowledge that while its value system may have been severely challenged, the status quo—the "norm" of its society—has been "reaffirmed by showing us what awful things happen to people who venture into taboo lands."[5]

The Shape of Contemporary American Horror

The contemporary horror tale is often distinguished from that of earlier generations in its representation of the female victim. Since its inception, the Gothic tale has evoked its thrills at the expense of women; traditionally, the Gothic heroine was the (present or future) wife of the hero. Her particular terror stimulated the Gothic villain's imagination as well as his libido and inspired the hero to a suitably heroic rescue. Thus, Isabella's fate and chastity are preserved in Walpole's *Castle of Otranto* through the intercession of Theodore; Mina Harker's virtues as both wife and Victorian woman are restored in Bram Stoker's *Dracula* through the efforts of her husband (Jonathan) and his male colleagues.

The contemporary Gothic female, on the other hand, must often confront the monster without the aid of a heroic male. In many horror stories, this nod towards feminism (a movement that is as often vilified as it is acknowledged in the genre) is mere window dressing—the unfolding narrative undercuts feminine independence and authority. Particularly in film, though, the heroine of horror must often call upon her own resources to vanquish the monster, restore the status quo, and survive.

In her discussion of gender dynamics in contemporary horror films, *Men, Women, and Chain Saws,* Carol Clover describes this shift towards independent resolve in the new Gothic heroine. Her observations about the "final girl" in slasher films apply elsewhere in contemporary horror art:

> By 1980, the male rescuer is either dismissably marginalized or dispensed with altogether; not a few films have him rush to the rescue only to be hacked to bits, leaving the Final Girl to save herself after all. At the moment that the Final Girl becomes her own savior, she becomes a hero; . . . Abject terror may still be gendered feminine, but the willingness of one immensely popular current genre to re-represent the hero as an anatomical female would seem to suggest that at least one of the traditional marks of heroism, triumphant self-rescue, is no longer strictly gendered masculine.[6]

In Stephen King's novels *Gerald's Game, Rose Madder,* and *Dolores Claiborne;* Christopher Fowler's "The Master Builder"; Thomas Harris's *The Silence of the Lambs;* and films such as *Alien* and *Halloween,* the female protagonist's courage and wits are severely tested. They remain her primary weapons against the intrusive force of the male monster. Her survival is tied directly to how well she employs them.

In addition to the evolving status of the horror maiden, the image of the contemporary monster has also undergone acute transformation. In horror prior to 1960, the monster rarely resembled a human being. There was always something to set him apart as Other: dress, body distortion, or animal appearance. Since then, however, the monster has been transformed into a "more human" representative; the tortured and torturing creatures of our time are less exotic than their predecessors. As Michael A. Morrison details in chapter 1, the omnipresent horror monster of the 1980s was the serial killer: seething on the inside, but one of us on the outside.

Ironically, the criminal sociopath establishes the closest affinity yet between audience and monster. Even as he preys upon us, he externalizes our awareness of imminent societal collapse, the demise of values, the illusoriness of security, and our rage at being unable to change any of this. The very randomness of the serial killer's choice of victims contrasts sharply with, for example, the design of revenge by Frankenstein's creature. To some extent, the serial killer embodies the haphazard scope of contemporary American life—our omnipresent anxieties over crime and violence, and the very anonymity of modern society itself.

Noël Carroll has proposed that contemporary horror differs from that of preceding generations, particularly in "descriptions and depictions of gore that go far beyond what one finds in the tradition."[7] This tendency might be explained in terms of the media assault that confronts Americans every day. We are subject to so many depictions of violence—both real and fictionalized—that we grow increasingly tolerant of its portrayal and presentation. The horror artist must then invent even more ghastly variations.

For some, this bloody contest signals the death of art and civilization; works of horror become a kind of postmodernist celebration of self-destruction, and the inadequacies of conceptional and ideological absolutes. But the horror aesthetic is more than simply a reaction to, or reflection of, nihilistic impulses in the self and society. Likewise, the art of horror, as distinguished from its mere exploitation, transcends physical descriptions of blood and guts, and cheap shock tricks. At its best, horror art is visionary and not reductive. It strips us of all that we know by challenging us to invent new categories and modes of comprehension. It tests and shakes our complacency as individuals and as members of a larger culture in order to force its protagonists and audience "to see the dark and explore the void beyond the face of order."[8] Its transformations are sometimes chaotic and frightening, but it can teach us much about ourselves and the world we are creating. We need only to possess the courage to look without flinching.

Notes

1. Leslie Fiedler, *Love and Death in the American Novel*, rev. ed. (New York: Stein & Day, 1966) 29.

2. Stephen King, *Danse Macabre*, rev. ed. (New York: Berkley, 1981) 26, 198.

3. Noël Carroll, *The Philosophy of Horror, or Paradoxes of the Heart* (New York: Routledge, 1990) 28.

4. Robin Wood, *Hollywood from Vietnam to Reagan* (New York: Columbia University Press, 1986) 84.

5. King 368.

6. Carol Clover, *Men, Women, and Chain Saws: Gender in the Modern Horror Film* (Princeton: Princeton University Press, 1992) 60.

7. Carroll 211.

8. Douglas E. Winter, "Introduction," *Prime Evil: New Stories by the Masters of Modern Horror* (New York: NAL, 1988) 8.

1

After the Danse
Horror at the End of the Century

Michael A. Morrison

> "Everything has a pattern,"
> Freddy put in.
> "If you can find it,
> the great can be contained
> within the small."
> —Clive Barker, *Weaveworld*

In *Danse Macabre* (1981), reigning horror master Stephen King informally surveyed the history of horror in our times. King's track of the changes in our culture's dark "dance with death" ends with 1980. But since then, horror has learned some new steps. The 1980s was an era of unprecedented growth and change for horror fiction. As King details, the current boom began in the late 1960s with the unexpected popularity of Ira Levin's *Rosemary's Baby* (1967), William Peter Blatty's *The Exorcist* (1971), and Thomas Tryon's *The Other* (1971). By 1987, horror was the fastest growing of the three imaginative genres, outpacing both science fiction and fantasy. During the contemporary era, roughly from the late 1970s through the early 1990s, horror mutated from a culturally disreputable backwater genre into a potentially lucrative marketing category—the commercial incarnation of what many consider the quintessential medium for our times. Horror titles regularly attained the status of best-sellers, and publishers like Bantam and Tor established designated horror lines—developments unthinkable a decade before. More to the point, during this period the nature of horror fiction changed decisively. Forces both financial and cultural wrought changes in the aesthetics and rhetoric of horror: in its balance of supernatural and nonsupernatural motifs; in its articulation of violence and the savagery beneath the civilized veneer of daily middle-class urban existence; and in its predominant literary form, which used to be the short story and now is the novel.

Whether one conceives of horror as a genre, a marketing category, or simply a collection of texts that share a common tonality, horror today is a literary mode that poses unique challenges to readers, publishers, and critics. Its singularly protean nature enables the appropriation and transmutation of materials from genres as diverse as science fiction, the romance novel, the western, and the spy thriller. This quality also facilitates its frequent incursions into the mainstream—where, in fact, horror has resided all along in works by Joyce Carol Oates, Ian McEwan, Scott Bradfield, and others. Especially during the 1980s, as writers toiled in the looming shadow of the horror bestseller, the field was so influenced by market forces that today it is almost impossible to consider its themes, tropes, or narrative strategies without dragging into the discussion the business of horror. At the same time, a variety of factors—some commercial, some artistic—have conspired to distribute the texts of horror throughout a maze of venues. For example, like science fiction, horror has always flourished in small-press magazines. But during the late 1980s, the fulminating horror underground served nurturing and generative functions far more important than did its counterpart in late twentieth-century science fiction. Merely accessing, let alone reading and assimilating, this unruly mass of often undistinguished fiction is, to say the least, daunting.

But such effort is essential. Even in this overview—a contextual frame for readers interested in, but not intimately familiar with, contemporary forms of the Gothic—it would not be sufficient to consider only the well-known works of Stephen King, Dean Koontz, Thomas Harris, Whitley Strieber, Anne Rice, and Peter Straub. Rather, one must also consider less familiar names and titles. A central premise of this perspective on modern horror fiction is that it defines itself not only in a small cluster of primary urtexts, but also in a huge number of variously accomplished novels and short stories that populate the mid-lists of hardcover publishers, racks of paperback originals, and small-press books and magazines.

This has not always been the case. As detailed in such histories as David Punter's *The Literature of Terror*, H. P. Lovecraft's *Supernatural Horror in Literature*, and Elizabeth MacAndrew's *The Gothic Tradition in Fiction*, the major developments of the classic period (during which the mode we now call horror fiction was born) took place in the works of a handful of writers: Mary Shelley, Ann Radcliffe, Bram Stoker, Robert Maturin, Ambrose Bierce, J. Sheridan Le Fanu, Henry James, and a few others. As S. T. Joshi's *The Weird Tale* and Julia Brigg's *Night Visitors* show, the premises and strategies of mid-twentieth-century weird and ghostly tales evolved largely in the fiction of Arthur Machen, Lord Dunsany, Edgar Allan Poe, Algernon Blackwood, M. R. James, and H. P. Lovecraft—all known primarily for their short fiction. But to render an accurate snapshot of horror at century's end, one must take into account not only *Ghost Story, The Silence of the Lambs, The Vampire Lestat* and *Dolores Claiborne,* but also the works of Thomas Ligotti, Dennis Etchison, Joe R. Lansdale, Charles L. Grant, Kathe Koja, and Nancy A. Collins—and of the cultural context in which these works were created and received. That context, primarily in its late-twentieth-century configuration, is the focus of the present essay.

Exploring in a few pages even a fraction of the thousands of horror stories, novellas, and novels published during the past twenty years poses obvious logistical problems. So the structure of this overview revolves around two primary polarities—necessarily exclusionary topics that focus issues and raise questions essential to understanding modern horror. First, the venues of horror: where is it regularly published, and how have these markets shaped the works they publish? Of its primary venues, the one that best illustrates the influence of market forces on literary matters—the content, form, and narrative strategies of modern horror—is the bestseller. The possibility that an appropriately configured horror novel might achieve the bestseller list has driven a number of developments during the 1980s, not the least of which is the clear preeminence of the novel. Equally important for wholly different reasons are the horror specialty presses—venues that throughout this period have played a catalytic role in the evolution of horror. The second focus is the dominant archetypes of modern horror: what are its most prominent recurrent monsters; how do they differ from their precursors (the creatures that stalked two centuries of earlier Gothic and ghostly fiction); and what does their recurring presence say to and about the culture that produces and receives them?

The Horror Bestseller and the Genre Hybrid

Throughout the 1980s, horror fiction appeared in four distinct venues: the bestselling hardcover, the mid-list hardcover, the paperback original, and the small-press product. Of these, the most prominent has been the hardcover book published by a major house (Doubleday, Viking, Knopf) explicitly aimed at the bestseller list. Of course, the horror bestseller is not unique to the 1980s. But what is unique is the contagion of "bestselleritis": the writing and marketing of a novel with the express intent of achieving huge sales. While according progenative status to a single work is risky, King's *'Salem's Lot* (1975) seems to have been the template—an influence Peter Straub, David Morrell, Al Sarrantonio, and others have acknowledged. King's successful fusion, in his first bestseller, of a familiar genre motif (the vampire) with the mainstream narrative strategies of popular fiction (the rural small-town soap opera) demonstrated the viability of a new—and potentially lucrative—kind of horror fiction.

In the wake of *'Salem's Lot* came a parade of aspiring horror bestsellers including Whitley Streiber's *The Wolfen* (1978), Peter Straub's *Ghost Story* (1979), Thomas Harris's *Red Dragon* (1981), F. Paul Wilson's *The Keep* (1981), T. E. D. Klein's *The Ceremonies* (1984), and George R. R. Martin's *The Armageddon Rag* (1984)—the list stretches into the 1990s with novels by Anne Rice, Robert R. McCammon, Clive Barker, Dan Simmons, John Saul, and Dean Koontz. All of these novels vary greatly in ambition and achievement—and many missed by a mile their target lists—but they share certain characteristics, narrative patterns, and strategies largely derived from popular nonhorror bestsellers by such writers as James Michener, Irving Wallace, and Robert Ludlum. Nearly all of these books aspire to a vast sweep and scope. Most are episodic and feature multiple plot lines constructed around standard genre tropes. Most strive to build suspense by refracting their plots through the viewpoints of several stereotypical characters. Most are over-insistently topical and densely peppered with explicit references to the popular culture of their times. And most are vehemently conservative, with narrative arcs and resolutions that eschew indeterminacy or long-term radical change from the status quo.

Perhaps the best example of the conscious crafting of one bestseller after another is Dean Koontz. Beginning in 1980 with *Whispers,* and continuing through a string of bestsellers up to *Mr. Murder* (1994) and *Dark Rivers of the Heart* (1995), Koontz has systematically refined a cluster of image patterns, character types, genre motifs, and plot structures into a formula for the very model of a modern major horror bestseller: male and female protagonists (usually unmarried) find fulfillment and renewal (and, in the process, save their community or, in some cases, the whole world) by defeating the menace—a bogey that is infrequently supernatural, sometimes extraterrestrial, and more often the spawn of his comicbook vision of "science gone wrong." Essential to the success of these novels is the "endangered child" (sometimes a pet serves as a surrogate child) who provides a focus for their efforts and emotions. Thus, in *Midnight* (1989), sinister computer mogul Thomas Shaddack has injected the entire population of the small California town of Midnight Cove with microchip "viruses" that enable the injectees to induce horrifying transformations. Two outsiders—an agent of the FBI and a plucky, irrepressible film producer—struggle to save themselves, an incredibly spunky young girl, the people of the town, and the rest of the world. During the odd quiet moment, these characters chat at length— elaborating Koontz's characteristically conservative message about the appalling state of the United States, the essential goodness of (some) human beings, and the importance of social responsibility.

To be sure, there is nothing wrong with crafting bestsellers—least of all novels as entertaining as many of Koontz's. For our purposes, "bestselleritis" is of interest because it has significantly altered the literary character and content of modern horror. In particular, this phenomenon has driven the preeminence of the novel over shorter forms, the propensity for novels that overtly incorporate elements of other genres into horror scenarios, and the shift in the locus of horror away from the supernatural.

As David Hartwell noted in his seminal "anatomy of horror," the anthology *The Dark Descent* (1987), during the 1980s the short story was superseded by the novel. Today, the short story remains vital and viable, but the novel reigns. On the one hand, the most innovative modern horror writers—Dennis Etchison, Thomas Ligotti, Douglas E. Winter, Michael Blumlein, Steve Rasnic Tem, Lisa Tuttle, and a few others— work exclusively, primarily, or most effectively in short forms. On the other hand, short-story collections (unless written by Stephen King) do not sell. Individually or in collections, short stories and novellas earn little money or attention. With the demise in the late 1980s of the two mainstream magazines devoted primarily to horror, *The Twilight Zone* and *Night Cry*, the only remaining short-story venues were the occasional original anthology, a few slots in *Fantasy and Science Fiction* and *Interzone*, and an indeterminate number of small-press magazines.

As illustrated by *The Dark Descent* and its successor, Hartwell's *Foundations of Fear* (1992), after the brief but intense reign of the British Gothic in the late eighteenth and early nineteenth centuries, horror became primarily a creature of the short form. During each of the major periods prior to the present, writers have found the concision and intensity of the short story, novelette, or novella most conducive to their aims. In the nineteenth century, E. Nesbit, W. W. Jacobs, Elizabeth Gaskell, and other British writers took advantage of the short story's intensity of focus to refine the mood and atmosphere of the Victorian ghost story. In the early twentieth century, Henry S. Whitehead, C. L. Moore, H. P. Lovecraft, and other American authors sought to liberate the horror short story from the rigid conventions of the American shudder pulps of the 1920s and 1930s. In later years, Richard Matheson, Charles Beaumont, Shirley Jackson, and other American masters of the short story experimented with the balance of detailed realistic settings and uncanny intrusions. And throughout the century, Walter de la Mare, Elizabeth Bowen, H. R. Wakefield, and other British writers introduced modernist strategies (such as subjective viewpoint and indeterminate resolution) into the British ghostly tale. This intensification of literary acumen culminated late in this century in the artistry of Ramsey Campbell, Nicholas Royle, Garry Kilworth, and Robert Aickman (to whom Peter Straub recently paid homage in his extraordinary novel *Mrs. God*. In each of these periods, then, writers developed the goals, aesthetics, and rhetorics of horror primarily in shorter forms.

Then came the bestselling novel. The long-term consequences of this change must not be underestimated. The novel—especially the long, character-packed, multiplot bestseller—tends to different agendas than does the short story. While the modern horror short story typically focuses on the psychology of a single character, the modern horror novel takes on society. And so we find social satire in many of King's works; inquiries into cultural definitions of evil in Thomas Harris's *The Silence of the Lambs* (1988) and Peter Straub's "Blue Rose" trilogy; probes of America's role in Vietnam in the stories collected by Jeanne Van Buren and Jack Dann in *In the Field of Fire* (1987); a critique of the sociopolitics of the AIDS epidemic in Dan Simmons's vampire novel *Children of the Night* (1992); gonzo metaphysical black comedy in Thomas M. Disch's *The Businessman: A Tale of Terror* (1984) and *The M.D.: A Horror Story* (1992); and elaborations of the tension between artistic and social responsibility in Jonathan Carroll's *A Child Across the Sky* (1989) and Giles Blunt's *Cold Eye* (1989). While the modern ghost story typically probes the boundary between the external and the internal or the real and the perceived, its novel-length counterpart tends primarily to the visceral, physical, and concrete. With notable exceptions like Thomas Tessier's *Phantom*

(1982), T. M. Wright's *The Playground* (1982), and T. L. Parkinson's *The Man Upstairs* (1991), the horror novel today assiduously avoids the narrow focus, subjectivity, and undecidability of the traditional ghostly tale.

Finally, and perhaps of greatest importance to the aesthetics of modern horror, the sustained character of the novel, which at its present length requires the attention of even the most obsessed and efficient reader for several sittings, precludes the type of affective response typically sought by short-story writers. That is, very few horror novels are scary. Perhaps to compensate, many of today's writers flesh out their novels with the paraphernalia of the everyday lives of their just-plain-folks characters. This relentless emphasis on the mundane often interferes with the delicate balance between realism and the fantastic—typical of the American horror short story in the past decades. From the late 1940s to the early 1960s, Richard Matheson, Robert Bloch, Charles Beaumont, Shirley Jackson, and others gradually shifted the focus of the horror story away from the essential weirdness of a supernatural manifestation (which had been the dominant preoccupation of the American horror pulp) to create the new American horror short story (which detailed the effect of eruptions of the uncanny or unnatural on recognizable middle-class characters into meticulously detailed realistic settings).

At their best, today's horror stories continue and enrich this tradition. Such novels as King's *Pet Sematary* (1983), Dennis Etchison's *Darkside* (1986), and Chet Williamson's *Ash Wednesday* (1987) elaborate convincing, compelling tales of ordinary men and women trapped and tested by extraordinary events—or, in the case of Dan Simmons's *Song of Kali* (1985), extraordinary settings. In these works, which tap a strain in American literature reaching back at least to the stories of Nathaniel Hawthorne, the supernatural and the horrific ironically challenge a character's capacity for moral choice and behavior. But at their worst, this tradition has been distorted in the fun-house mirror of the modern bestseller—the delicate balance between realism and the fantastic deformed in vast, irredeemably mundane narratives punctuated by presumably frightening (but usually merely gross) set pieces. The effect is not fear, but tedium.

So the preeminence of the novel during the 1980s—a consequence of marketing concerns, in general, and the seductive lure of bestsellerdom, in particular—has reconfigured the ends and means of horror. Further driving this reconfiguration is one of the strengths of modern horror: its almost limitless malleability. To the extent that, as Douglas E. Winter has articulated in an informal panel discussion at the International Conference on the Fantastic in the Arts, in Boca Raton, Florida, in 1992, horror is an emotion, it can appropriate material from any other literary mode or genre. Indeed, the very capaciousness of the novel offers space for the interplay of elements across the permeable membrane of genre. Moreover, cross-generic novels have demonstrated appeal to the mass readership. During the 1980s, horror writers increasingly adopted the literary tactic of genre splicing.

The up-market horror hybrid, which must have the feel of a bestseller, often identifies itself as horror primarily by the presence of a genre trope. In the works of Anne Rice, one finds witches in *The Witching Hour* (1990) and *Lasher* (1993); mummies in *The Mummy, or Ramses the Damned* (1989); and vampires in four novels of *The Vampire Chronicles* (1976, 1985, 1988, and 1992). In these and many other bestsellers, horror motifs are variously enhanced or undercut by juxtaposition with elements from other genres; Rice's use of the family chronicle in *The Witching Hour* works, her use of the romance in *The Mummy* does not. Nevertheless, the success of genre splicing in attracting a large readership—and the artistic and thematic expansion it offers—have proven irresistible. So one finds genre melds in innumerable other aspiring bestsellers: the coming-of-age novel in Tryon's *The Night of the Moonbow* (1989), the chase thriller in McCammon's *Mine* (1990) and the World-War II espionage adventure in *The Wolf's Hour* (1989), the detective thriller in Thomas Harris's *Red Dragon* (1981) and *The Silence of the Lambs* (1988), the paranoid science fiction story in Koontz's *Cold Fire* (1991) and King's *The Tommyknockers* (1987), the techno-thriller and police procedural in Christopher Fowler's *Rune* (1990), and the multigenerational family chronicle in Michael McDowell's six-novel saga *Blackwater* (1983).

But genre splicing is by no means restricted to the blockbuster bestseller. Throughout the decade, the genre blend has percolated in the other major venues for horror: the mid-list hardcover, the paperback original, and the small-press publication. Just next door, in the mainstream literary novel, Patrick McGrath, Dennis Cooper, Paul West, Joyce Carol Oates, Paul Theroux, Emmanual Carrére, Valerie Martin, Eric McCormack, and others have unselfconsciously infused materials from other genres into horror scenarios. But it is in the down-market paperback original that one finds the most bizarre outgrowth: whole subgenres created entirely through hybridization. By far the most popular subgenre of modern horror, the tale of the vampire, has spawned such sub-subgenres as the vampire police procedural, a form prefigured in Leslie Whitten's *Progeny of the Adder* (1965) and realized in modern terms in Stephen Gallagher's *Valley of Lights* (1988); the vampire-hard-boiled-detective story, as realized by *The Vampire Files*, P. N. Elrod's six-novel series set in depression-era Chicago; the historical vampire novels of Chelsea Quinn Yarbro's multivolume *Chronicles of St. Germain* and Les Daniels's novels featuring Don Sebastian de Villaneuva; and the vampire rock-and-roll novel, as exemplified by Nancy A. Collins's *Tempter* (1990), Poppy Z. Brite's *Lost Souls* (1992), and S. P. Somtow's *Vampire Junction* (1984).

Not unexpectedly, this sort of thing can get out of hand. For instance Jack Butler's enjoyable novel, *Nightshade* (1989) features a vampire secret agent in a cyberpunk Western set on twenty-first-century Mars, and John Steakley's considerably less enjoyable soldier-of-fortune horror novel, *Vampire$* (1990) offers a gun-toting paramilitary SWAT team that strives to protect the elite of society from infestation by vampires. As Butler's *Nightshade* illustrates, the genre that has supplied horror with its richest and most malleable material is science fiction. In each year since the late 1970s, novels and short stories have explored the interface between horror and science fiction by interfusing ideas, tropes, and motifs from science fiction with the scenarios, atmospherics, and monsters of horror fiction. The results range from the sublime to the very very silly. In the best science fiction/horror novels—Dan Simmons's *Carrion Comfort* (1989), Brian Stableford's *The Empire of Fear* (1988), Kim Newman's *The Night Mayor* (1989), and Peter Ackroyd's *First Light* (1989), to name a few—writers find in the tension between these two essentially different literary modes a peculiar narrative energy unavailable to either mode separately. Thus, Ackroyd's novel blends science fiction, myth, astrology, and archaeology in a Hardyesque tale about the excavation of an ancient cairn in modern England. His achievement, which evidently baffled many mainstream reviewers, becomes clear in the context of American Gothic: *First Light* deftly inverts the premises of Lovecraftian cosmic horror even as it preserves their metaphysical *frisson*.

Failed science fiction/horror hybrids, of course, far outnumber such successes. These novels often stumble over their authors' inability to fuse cleanly generic and extra-generic elements. This problem defeats writers at all levels of craft and success: Dean Koontz's awkward use of

teleportation and telepathy in *The Bad Place* (1988) and time-travel paradoxes in his horror romance *Lightning* (1988); and Alan Rodgers's inept
appropriation of post-apocalyptic scenarios in his ostensible epic *Fire*
(1989), which at times reads like a gonzo camp pastiche of Robert R.
McCammon's more successful *Swan Song* (1987) and Stephen King's
much more successful *The Stand* (1978, rev. 1990). At their worst, failed
science fiction/horror hybrids are merely risible—a memorable case-in-
point being Garfield Reeve-Steven's *Dark Matter* (1990), which features
a Nobel prize-winning theoretical physicist who strives to apprehend the
secrets of the quantum universe by vivisecting women.

From the perspective of the mid-1990s, the shift during the previous
decade from short fiction to the novel as the predominant form for horror
appears crucial but not definitive. This shift illustrates that real-time
interconnections between the Gothic, the market, and the culture that
produces and receives horror fiction are so intimate and so intricate as to
render this mode essentially unstable in both content and form. During
recent years the balance has shifted somewhat back to shorter forms.
Numbers continue to favor the novel. But during the first few years
of the 1990s, an old publishing form took advantage of the absence of
mainstream magazines to assume new prominence: the anthology. Every
year of the decade saw increasing numbers of original anthologies both
in the genre and well outside it; thus, in 1991 there appeared Charles
L. Grant's *Final Shadows;* Bradford Morrow and Patrick McGrath's *The
New Gothic;* Alfred Birnbaum's *Monkey Brain Sushi;* and Thomas Colchie's *A Hammock Beneath the Mangoes*. Accompanying these catch-all
anthologies and the ever-present single-author collections were theme
anthologies, which highlighted a common trope or theme (such as the
haunted house, the werewolf, or sex) and shared-world anthologies
(which featured stories set in a common world or locale). Thus, all the
stories in Charles L. Grant's four-volume *Graystone Bay* series were set
in the eponymous town, while those in John Skipp and Craig Spector's
two-volume *Book of the Dead* series were set in a future first posited in
George Romero's seminal 1968 horror film *Night of the Living Dead*.
Alongside such original collections were increasing numbers of reprint
anthologies, which have restored to print much of the tradition of the
Gothic and supernatural—a tradition of which too many contemporary
writers are ignorant. Many of these books appeared from mainstream
presses such as Morrow, St. Martin's Press, and Pantheon that years
earlier had shunned horror anthologies. By the mid-1990s, the real action
had left the mainstream altogether.

Into the Small Presses Ghetto

Far from the limelight of the elaborately engineered, potentially bestselling horror genre, one can find the horror specialty publishers. Unknown except to a small cadre of aficionados, small presses throughout the century have nurtured all modes of the fantastic—from the Munsey magazines and other amateur publications of H. P. Lovecraft's day to now legendary specialty publishers like Fantasy Press, Gnome Press, and the still active Arkham House (which in 1993 celebrated its fifty-fifth year of publication). During the last half of the twentieth century, small presses played a distinctive, singularly important, and often unappreciated role in horror fiction.

The 1960s and 1970s were the dog days of the Gothic. Magazine venues that for decades had regularly published horror were gone. Mainstream publishers shunned it; paperback publishers emphasized science fiction, realistic popular fiction, and the perennial romance novel; and the public seemed uninterested. Indeed, horror survived and continued to grow during these decades largely in a few persistent, high-quality small-press magazines—notably Stuart Schiff's *Whispers*, Paul Ganley's *Weirdbook*, and David B. Silva's *The Horror Show*. Then, with the post-1970s horror boom, the small-press magazine market exploded. At its peak, around 1986, this market spawned *Grue*, *2AM*, *Footsteps*, *Horrorstruck*, *New Blood*, *Twisted*, and *Midnight Grafitti*. Later, such magazines as *Pulphouse*, *The Blood Review*, *Deathrealm*, *Scream Factory*, *Cemetary Dance*, and others appeared.

In the history of horror in the 1980s, small-press magazines commanded attention for the myriad roles they played. Distinguished by their editors' seemingly boundless energy and fierce commitment, these magazines thrived in spite of ludicrously small budgets. In issue after issue, appearing on schedules as erratic as their contents, they offered a training field for Thomas Ligotti, Richard Christian Matheson, Wayne Allen Sallee, David J. Schow, Poppy Z. Brite, Nina Kiriki Hoffman, Kathe Koja, and many new writers who later graduated to the proving ground of mainstream publishing. Their eclecticism and liberal policies made small-press magazines ideal venues for experimental or otherwise uncommercial work—an opportunity seized by Joe R. Lansdale, Lucius Shephard, Fred Chappel, Ramsey Campbell, Stephen King, and many other well-established writers. Almost exclusively, the small-press ghetto offered a home to the rare story that dared counter the prevailing conservatism of mainstream horror—publishing, for example, innovative short fiction by Douglas E. Winter, T. Winter-Damon, Michael Blumlein, and Thomas Ligotti, and novels by S. P. Somtow and Scott Edelman. Finally, these presses provided continuing venues for exceptional works by such writers as Steve Rasnic Tem, Dennis Etchison, Karl Edward Wagner, and poets such as Bruce Boston and Robert Frazier—artists who, largely because of the uncommercial status of poetry and short stories, could not regularly publish outside the specialty presses.

Not surprisingly, the profligacy of magazines in the 1980s could not be sustained either with dollars from the readership or quality stories from the writers. As the decade waned, so did the small presses. Editorial laxity, a propensity by young writers to fill their stories with gratuitous graphic gore, and the incestuous editorial policies of a few journals conspired with a publishing recession to all but destroy the small-press magazine. Most of the magazines noted above are gone; those that remain publish little of interest.

In the arid ground of glut and recession, a new and even more important role for the specialty presses was born. As mainstream publishers shrank their lists of horror books, the small presses took up the slack. New presses such as CD Publications, ESA Books, Silver Salamander Press, Dark Harvest, TAL, John Maclay, Roadkill Press, Fedogen and Bremer, Borderlands Press, Twilight Publishing, Dark Regions Press, and others joined venerable old-timers Mark V. Ziesing, Arkham House, Donald E. Grant, and Marc Michaud of Necronomicon Press. And, by 1993, almost 25 percent of all new horror novels, anthologies, and collections appeared from a specialty press.

In the 1990s, the horror small presses are more diverse than ever. Some regularly publish limited first editions of major novels and sole hardcovers of others. In 1993, Mark V. Ziesing published Peter Straub's *The Throat;* in 1994, Stephen King's *Insomnia* (both of which later appeared in trade hardcover); and, in 1993, Lucius Shepard's *The Golden* (which later appeared only in a mass-market paperback). Others publish original anthologies either singly or in series such as Dark Harvest's *Dark Visions* and Borderlands Press *Borderlands*. Others often feature novellas by such well-known writers as Shepard, Michael Shea, Fred Chappel, and Harlan Ellison. And, as in previous decades, most major presses sometimes produce single-author collections. During the late 1980s, for example, there appeared collections by well-known writers such as Joe R. Lansdale, Pat Caddigan, and John Shirley, and newcomers such as

Poppy Z. Brite, Michael Blumlein, and Clive Barker (whose first three *Books of Blood* were published in 1985 by Scream/Press). By the mid-1990s, the single-author collection, now usually in the form of a small chapbook, had become the dominant form of small-press publication; 1993 alone saw chapbooks by Elizabeth Massie, Mark Rainey, Adam de Troy Castro, Lucy Taylor, Donald Burleson, Michael Arnzen, Albert J. Manachino, Ken Wieman, Wayne Allan Sallee, Brett Rutherford, D. F. Lewis, and others.

That most of these names are unfamiliar is precisely the point. Even as American Gothic thrives and evolves in the small presses, it does so largely unseen. Even in the heyday of the specialty press, very little of its product survived the American distribution network to reach the audience it deserved. Now, a partial solution exists in the form of easily available annual "best of" anthologies. Of these anthologies, the longest lived and most eclectic is *The Year's Best Horror Stories*, which in 1994 published its 22nd installment. Under the astute editorship of Karl Edward Wagner from 1980 until his death in 1994, this series constitutes the essential history of the horror story in our time. Augmenting Wagner's annual is its sibling series, *Best New Horror*, edited by Stephen Jones and Ramsey Campbell (vol. 4, 1993) and *The Year's Best Fantasy and Horror* edited by Ellen Datlow and Terri Windling (vol. 7, 1994).

Valuable as these compendia are, they only hint at the energy and innovation that surges through small-press venues. Perhaps the most significant developments in the small-press ghetto are less the efforts of individual writers than the collective cultural excavation they have undertaken. Unfettered by editorial restraint or the need to please a potentially large readership, small-press writers (good, bad, and indifferent) are exposing fears that percolate below the surface of our millennial culture—fears that have yet to emerge in the mainstream literary landscape.

The Archetypes of Modern Horror

Identifying cultural fears already abroad in American popular culture requires only a keen eye, a tolerance for trash, and a knack for the translation of tropes. Good or bad, most late-twentieth-century horror tales feature monsters akin to the creatures that populated horror stories of the eighteenth and nineteenth centuries. Of the many fantastic beings that have stalked the pages of horror from the late eighteenth century to the present, only a few possessed sufficient adaptability and metaphoric power to detach from their source texts and enter the cultural myth pool. These are the archetypes of horror—the links in the chain of literary tradition of terror and the supernatural.

The chain of horror archetypes reaches from Horace Walpole's progenative eighteenth-century Gothic *The Castle of Otranto* (1754) to Thomas Harris's seminal serial-killer novel *The Silence of the Lambs* (1988). The classic Gothic novel featured the vampire, the eternal wanderer (Melmoth and his literary kin), and the "thing without a name" (Frankenstein's monster and others). The late-Victorian short story gave top billing to the revenant and the human monster Jekyll/Hyde. Early in the twentieth century, these and other bogeys shambled through the American shudder pulps along with two newcomers—the extraterrestrial and the Lovecraftian cosmic monster. Late-twentieth-century Gothic both transforms older archetypes and breeds its own. The evil child, the psychically over-endowed adolescent, the shapeshifter, the anti-Christ, and especially the zombie and the serial killer are featured in a seemingly endless profusion of texts that demonstrate an almost limitless adaptability of motifs. Of all these traditional and contemporary figures, the vampire and the serial killer most clearly exemplify current propensities in modern horror and their attendant problems.

About the literary vampire we need say little. He (it is almost always a he) has been a monster in good standing since his birth in Polidori's early nineteenth-century tale "The Vampyre," Thomas Prescott Prest's 1840 penny dreadful *Varney the Vampire* (1840), and his coming of age in the great vampire urtext, Bram Stoker's *Dracula* (1897). Today, the vampire is omnipresent both within and outside the horror genre. Originally of rural origin, he now stalks environments from small towns to great cities around the world. In the years since Richard Matheson exploded the metaphor of the vampire in his 1954 novel *I Am Legend*, the play of repetition and variation in stories featuring this robust motif has produced an almost limitless variety—including forms Stoker would doubtless have found appalling: the immortal teenage rockstar of S. P. Somtow's *Vampire Junction* (1984) and its sequel *Valentine* (1992), or the vampire hookers of Ray Garton's *Live Girls* (1987). The most interesting modern treatments of this archetype generalize it into metaphor. In *Carrion Comfort* (1989), the *Moby Dick* of vampire novels, Dan Simmons uses vampirism as a metaphor for the objectification and dehumanization that accompany personal or political power over others. And in his century-spanning cross-cultural scientific romance, *The Empire of Fear* (1988), Brian Stableford uses the vampire myth to foreground epistemological issues that arise from the entire skein of legends that comprise the human heritage of the fantastic.

Commentators often wonder at the enormous popularity of the literary vampire. To be sure, some credit must go to Anne Rice. But the appeal of the vampire ranges beyond her achievements. Perhaps an explanation can be excavated from Ellen Datlow's recent anthologies, *Blood Is Not Enough* (1989) and *A Whisper of Blood* (1990), in which various contributors elaborated the metaphor of vampirism into a startling variety of predator-victim relationships. If, as Frank McConnel observes in *The Spoken Seen* (1975), "each era chooses the monster it deserves and projects," then maybe it is not so hard to understand why a creature that subsists on the lives of others would appeal to a culture whose primary discourse is the politics of victimization.

The theme of victimization also empowers the other dominant late-twentieth-century horror archetype—the serial killer. Contrasts between this literary motif and the vampire highlight two key facets of modern horror. First, the serial killer is primarily urban (an embodiment of the fear of random violence that now defines city life). Second, he (rarely she) is not supernatural. In this second respect, the serial killer typifies perhaps the most significant thematic shift in modern Gothic. In the late 1970s, supernatural horror moved decisively from the classic tradition of ambiguous manifestations, usually rooted in character psychology, to the modern tradition of explicitly physical ghosts. But in the late 1980s, the horror novel moved within the mode of visceral terror away from the supernatural altogether. A long list of writers—including King, Straub, McCammon, Joe R. Lansdale, Stephen Gallagher, and others—began their careers writing supernatural novels but have largely abandoned them in favor of nonsupernatural scenarios such as the police procedural, crime noir, suspense thriller, or the detective story. So prominent have such scenarios become that by the mid-1990s a new subgenre had emerged—christened the "dark suspense."

Although anticipated by earlier psychological suspense-horror novels such as Robert Bloch's *Psycho* (1959) and Ramsey Campbell's *The Face that Must Die* (1979), the serial-killer genre of the 1980s erupted full-grown from three books published in 1988: Thomas Harris's *The Silence of the Lambs,* Peter Straub's *Koko,* and David Schow's *The Kill Riff.* Harris complicates, blurs, and renders human the traditional horror polarities of good and evil in order to illustrate the difficulty of defining and recognizing either in the modern world—and the consequent danger of inadvertently compromising innocence and nurturing evil. Straub, in the first volume of his "Blue World" trilogy, locates the wellspring of modern evil in the Vietnam War and uses the overworked figure of the psychotic Vietnam veteran to problematize the quest for values in a world devoid of moral absolutes. And Schow spins a grim, compelling narrative set in the rock music industry around the idea that deficient social values and our culture's obsession with image and opinion can encourage acceptance and even nurturance of monsters in our midst. The serial killer today is so powerfully resonant that he has starred in recent literary slasher novels such as Paul Theroux's *Chicago Loop,* Dennis Cooper's *Frisk,* and Bret Easton Ellis's notorious *American Psycho* (all 1991).

In the few short years since that watershed, a torrent of largely inept and vacuous serial-killer novels have all but exhausted this motif. Nonsupernatural creatures lack attributes that enlarge and empower narratives about supernatural beings: their potential for ambiguity, their metaphorical resonance, and their access to a reader's sense of the numinous and transcendent. The serial killer tends to slash his way through the surface of narrative—vivifying in text rather than subtext the fears of the culture. The serial-killer novel brings to the surface the pervasive paranoia that underpins most modern horror, where we are all potential victims trapped in inherently uncontrollable natural or technological environments, within a cosmos that is at best indifferent. Most such works display an appalling atrophy of the imagination. Their authors seem to operate on the assumption that the mere mention of a psychopath or serial killer, accompanied by graphic renderings of diverse atrocities, suffices to make a successful horror novel. Lacking either subtext or subtlety, these novels amount to the literary equivalents of *Friday the Thirteenth* movies. Notable recent exceptions include Ramsey Campbell's *The Count of Eleven* (1991), Bradley Denton's *Blackburn* (1993), and Andrew Vachss's *Shella* (1993). These novels attain substance by challenging the very knee-jerk reactions that lesser novels exploit. Campbell renders his serial-killer scenario as slapstick comedy, while Denton and Vachss evoke complex responses by shading the serial killer's motivations and contexts, thus making them less monochromatically evil.

American Gothic

One must not underestimate the range and resonance of horror fiction for late-twentieth-century America. Many critics have elaborated King's observation in *Danse Macabre* (20) that an important role of disreputable genres like horror is exposing and exploring anxieties that course beneath the surface of the daily life and realistic literature of a nation—those "phobic pressure points" that, in King's words, "are so deeply buried and yet so vital that [horror writers] may tap them like artesian wells—saying one thing out loud while we express something else in a whisper." Writers of each generation mold the conventions and traditions of the Gothic to their own articulation of the subcultural fears of their times. Hence, midcentury novels contain such archetypes as the evil child, the small-town terror, satanic survivals, and invasions of various body snatchers, while more recent tales feature techno-horror, child abuse, the monstrous yuppie, the apocalypse, the vampire, and the serial killer.

Traditionally, mainstream fiction (literary and otherwise) has told of optimism and innocence—the tale of the American dream; horror tells its obverse—the American nightmare. Casting a pessimistic eye on the avowed innocence and promise of the American establishment, the writers of horror have sought the means to vivify the dark underside of the American dream in the Gothic.

In one sense, of course, this is nothing new in American fiction. As Tony Magistrale has explored in a series of books on the works of Stephen King, American writers from Hawthorne to King have found in horror not the limited means of an inferior genre, but an essential mode of perception and representation—the Gothic viewpoint that Melville called (in a review of Hawthorne's *Mosses from an Old Manse* [1846]) "the power of blackness."

In another sense, however, horror fiction is unique to our age. Perhaps no writer better exemplifies the distinctively contemporary American appropriation of the Gothic outlook than Dennis Etchison. Primarily (and most successfully) a writer of short stories—gathered in the collections *The Dark Country* (1982), *Red Dreams* (1984), and *The Blood Kiss* (1984)—Etchison eschews vampires, werewolves, and the like for the pain of here and now. His stories reveal a preoccupation with the homogenizing, debilitating culture of the West and the spiritual zombies who drift through it—concerns that place Etchison firmly in a current of American fiction that runs from Nathaniel West to Thomas McGuane.

His style could not be farther from the genre "norm." Unlike most of his contemporaries, Etchison constructs narratives of elliptical structures and oblique angles in spare, introspective, and almost impressionistic prose. But his stories are unmistakably horror fiction. Empowered by subtle allusions and potent metaphors that reshape the traditions of the Gothic, these stories often return to a single theme: the origin of the void at the heart of American life in the experience of loss. Works such as "The Olympic Runner" (1986), "Home Call" (1983), and "The Dark Country" (1981), "Deathtracks" (1981) expose the darkest corners of man-made America—its cities and the enclaves of civilization that dot the wilderness.

In their works, Etchison, Straub, Simmons, King, Rice, and Strieber continue to demonstrate the viability, malleability, resonance, and relevance of the mode of Gothic horror to our times. These works show that in spite of the superficiality and repetitiveness found in much of modern horror, in spite of its often pointlessly unpleasant imagery, and in spite of sporadic outbreaks of "bestselleritis" and the consequent engorgement of the horror novel—horror is not moribund. These stories and novels further show that the face of modern horror is changing. Its continual metamorphosis through ongoing dialogues with other genres and with the mainstream make horror today less a category or genre than a mode of perception. The American novel, as Leslie Fiedler has taught us, is preeminently a novel of terror. And our culture's fascination with horror continues to the present, as writers old and new invite us to one last dance with our own darkest demons.

Note

I am deeply grateful to my valued friends Stefan Dziemianowicz, Michael J. Collins, Douglas E. Winter, and Tony Magistrale for their insightful critical writings on horror fiction and for their willingness to discuss at length the many issues that surround the fiction of terror and the supernatural, all of which helped immeasurably in the shaping of many of the ideas in this essay.

2

Transmogrified Gothic
The Novels of Thomas Harris

Tony Magistrale

. . . when the Male & Female
Appropriate Individuality, they become an Eternal Death.
Hermaphroditic worshippers of a God of cruelty & law!
—William Blake, *Jerusalem*

In his intriguing study of Gothic film and literature, *Dreadful Pleasures: An Anatomy of Modern Horror,* James Twitchell argues that our attraction to the art of terror is essentially psychosexual: "Horror has little to do with fright; it has more to do with laying down the rules of socialization and extrapolating a hidden code of sexual behavior."[1] Twitchell's thesis is very helpful in providing a Freudian model for viewing the genre, particularly in understanding its relevance to an adolescent audience engaged in the complicated and sometimes terrifying transition to adulthood. Perhaps the most provocative corollary to this analysis, however, occurs late in his book when Twitchell addresses the structural prototypes of Gothic art. In his chapter on Stevenson's *Dr. Jekyll and Mr. Hyde,* Twitchell postulates that the horror genre has always revolved around concepts and images of transformation—shape changing—whether psychological, physical, or both. Mr. Hyde, the Frankenstein creature, the Wolfman, and the vampire all share a common lineage: the acting out of taboo behavior once the polite, socially acceptable human being has been displaced by the monster.

Thomas Harris's three novels—*Black Sunday* (1975), *Red Dragon* (1981), and *The Silence of the Lambs* (1988)—are all in keeping with the

Gothic tradition Twitchell defines; they are each, to lesser or greater degrees, books that highlight characters undergoing identity transitions and transmogrifications. And like the Jekyll/Hyde paradigm, the characters in Harris who are most involved with physical transformation also view their change in self-transcendent terms. Jekyll comes to recognize that the Hyde part of his personality is not only more physically dominant, but more psychologically compelling. In *Black Sunday,* the Black September terrorists are willing to sacrifice individual lives—their own included—for the sake of a political cause that has consumed them; the death of thousands at the Super Bowl becomes a radical but necessary prerequisite toward transforming society. Similarly, in the stripping away of former selves, to be replaced by some new physical being perhaps imagined but never actualized, Francis Dolarhyde in *Red Dragon* and Jame Gumb in *The Silence of the Lambs* may be likened to the Black September group insofar as they all seek liberation in violence against an indifferent society. These characters share a philosophy of obsession: for them, Twitchell's "projection of repressed desire,"[2] whether it serves a personal or political agenda, can only occur through the violent imposition of one will over another.

Red Dragon

William Blake's painting *The Great Red Dragon and the Woman Clothed with the Sun* is the dominant symbol for Dolarhyde's process of "becoming" in the novel *Red Dragon.* As is often the case in Blake's watercolors, the painting highlights the emergence of the man-God (a vision of the imagination made tangible and direct). Dolarhyde writes to Hannibal Lecter hoping the incarcerated psychiatrist will recognize the visionary dimension of Dolarhyde's "becoming." In this correspondence he refers to himself as "Pilgrim," indicating his acute self-awareness of his role as an explorer engaged in a transcendant journey. Like Blake's conception of the artist, Dolarhyde views himself as a man pressing, with the full power of his aroused creativity, against the walls of obedience and restraint.

Dolarhyde's first exposure to a reproduction of Blake's painting initiates a personal identification with the figure of the demonic dragon hovering over the figure of a terrified woman: "He carried the picture with him for days, photographed and enlarged it in the darkroom late at night. . . . With the fervor of conversion he saw that if he worked at

it, if he followed the true urges he had kept down for so long—culti-
vated them as the inspirations they truly were—he could Become."[3] At
least half of *Red Dragon* concerns the gradual unfolding of exactly what
Dolarhyde wishes to become; Blake's watercolor, which Dolarhyde
eventually eats in an effort to subsume the painting's potency, appears
to connect directly with Dolarhyde's transformative urge to assume the
role of masculine avenger. As Stevenson's Hyde assumes and abuses the
privileges of patriarchal control and physical dominance, so does Francis
Dolarhyde view the process of his own "becoming" (the "hyde" of Dolarhyde perhaps a direct allusion to Stevenson's earlier creature). Blake's
painting portrays "the Man-Dragon rampant over the prostrate pleading
woman caught in a coil of his tail";[4] correspondingly, Dolarhyde's metamorphosis revolves around the accumulation of power at the expense of
women. He appears to measure the level of his "becoming" by forcing
women into the simultaneous roles of adoring spectators and sacrificial
victims.

His own self-delusions notwithstanding, Dolarhyde's obsessive need
to become something else—a Blakean concept beyond traditional moral
codes, societal restraints, or even human recognition—suggests the extent of his own self-hatred. True to the romantic code of art born of
human anguish, Blake's paintings and poetry frequently juxtapose suffering with a transcendant consciousness. As Mario Praz argues in *The
Romantic Agony*, "For the Romantics beauty was enhanced by exactly
those qualities which seem to deny it, by those objects which produce
horror; the sadder, the more painful it was, the more intensely they
relished it."[5] Born into a world where he has known only exclusion and
humiliation, Dolarhyde punishes women at the same time as he seeks
their veneration. Women are an incessant reminder, in their sexual rejection, of his own physical deformity and, equally as important, of the
childhood abandonment by his mother. His violence can be seen, in
part, as violence against himself, or at least against that part of himself
that he is desperate to forsake. This is why Dolarhyde is interested only
in women victims (he virtually ignores their husbands and children). Female eyes that once averted their gaze and mouths that once uttered
patronizing words are now filled with, and project, the emerging physical
images of Dolarhyde's "becoming." The dead women are at the center
of a ritualized ceremony; they assume the role of the prostrate female in
Blake's painting or of a participant in the numinous experience: blinded
by the dragon-god's emergence and struck dumb in transfixed awe.

Blake wrote and drew from a fathomless inner window through

which he attempted to discover radical insights. As Alfred Kazin observes, "Blake then used the thing created—the poem, the picture, joined in their double vision—as a window in itself, through which to look to what was still beyond."[6] "I look through the eye," Blake said in words that would have meant everything to Francis Dolarhyde, "not with it." Like Blake's Satan in *The Marriage of Heaven and Hell*, Dolarhyde lives to destroy individual lives, but he believes their destruction to be a source of energy—opening vistas to new worlds induced by transcendant transformation. As Blake acknowledged, a person's true nature could be discovered only by pursuing "the lineaments of Gratified Desire"; destruction was necessary to release the full power of a person's creative will to assert and transform. Similarly, "Dolarhyde knew the unreality of the people who die to help you in these things—understood that they are not flesh, but light and air and color and quick sounds quickly ended when you change them. . . . Dolarhyde bore screams as a sculptor bears dust from the beaten stone."[7] Most importantly, Dolarhyde's ritualized actions put him in contact with a beautiful, although dead, female audience no longer capable of rejecting him. The fact that his ritual is highly choreographed, and then scrupulously critiqued during his later reviews of the videotape, indicates that Dolarhyde is obsessed with his new emergent identity; the act of watching his own "becoming" reveals his essential link to the protean energies inherent in Blake's creation myths.

The irony ultimately inherent in Dolarhyde's quest is that he reduces Blake's evocative symbols of the visionary human imagination to mere acts of degrading butchery; his dragon-man alter ego revels in attacking helpless women and children who are asleep. A more sophisticated and accurate response to Blake, including his many endeavors to contrapose gender stereotyping, opposes what Dolarhyde interprets from his work. As Mary Lynn Johnson argues, most of Blake's poems and watercolors "present an unsparing critique of a male-dominated world order and an androcentric value system."[8] Blake's art epitomizes the positive attributes of breaking free from the oppressive social veneers of everyday life. In his need to tyrannize others in order to achieve his own sense of freedom, Dolarhyde certainly misapprehends Blake, but nowhere in the novel does Harris acknowledge this misapprehension. Is this because the writer is reluctant to become an intrusive presence in the narrative by balancing the reductive thinking of his unbalanced character? Or does Harris mean to indict Blake by twisting and critiquing the naive and destructive potential inherent in the romantic urge to recreate the self? I would suggest that the latter is the more compelling of these two speculations; moreover, its self-encoded explanation represents the essential separation between Gothicism and romantic optimism. Whereas Blake and other romantics understood that freedom from social, political, and ethical codes of conduct would produce true individuals capable of realizing their divine potential, the Gothic romance marked a shift from faith in human nature to moral skepticism. The Gothic, and here the fiction of Thomas Harris would seem to concur most completely, has always challenged humankind's capacity for balancing forces of good and evil—further suggesting that when their impulses remained unchecked humans were more likely to perform acts of perversity than poetry.

The Silence of the Lambs

It is crucial to keep in mind Dolarhyde's inimitable desire-aversion conflict in his attitude toward women if we are to understand the similar psychopathology at work in *The Silence of the Lambs*. Like *Red Dragon*, *Silence* is about the evolutionary process of "becoming." Although Jame Gumb shares with Dolarhyde a definition of the self engaged in a glorious transition, his metamorphosis is no less monstrous. The serial killers in each book require the ritualized slaying of women to enact their respective changes. Dolarhyde appears to be interested in securing some level of homage or acceptance from the women he selects, while Jame Gumb (known as Buffalo Bill) sees women only as "its": physical beings selected purely for the quality of their skins. Dolarhyde thinks himself to be the apotheosis of masculinity, while Gumb identifies with the feminine. In addition to adhering to stereotypical, one-dimensional gender definitions, both suffer from severe mother fixations and complexes. Dolarhyde desires to transform his female victims into mother-surrogates exulting in the birth of a beautiful son, while Gumb actually seeks to recreate the image of his own mother in himself.

The biological advance of the death-head moth—from larva, to pupa, to emerging adult—is a metaphor for Jame Gumb's transmogrification from male into female. Early on we learn, for example, that the moth is clearly linked to Gumb's stalking; there are some moths who live entirely on "the tears of large land mammals, about our size. The old definition of moth was 'anything that gradually, silently eats, consumes, or wastes any other thing.' It was a verb for destruction too."[9]

Buffalo Bill not only feasts on the wasted "tears" of his victims who must be destroyed for their "pelts", but he is also crying for himself: his own tears of pain and frustration over years of entrapment in a male body. His victims, like Dolarhyde's, are necessary, though expendable, elements leading to the realization of a new self.

Gumb's journey to femininity descends into the realm of the grotesque. He believes that becoming female is merely a matter of physiological disguising (or assuming the form). Of course, the issue of what it means to be female is as much spiritual and psychological as it is physical. As statistics on serial killers confirm, men commit these acts; women do not systematically murder and skin other human beings. Jame Gumb's quest to become a female is ironically thwarted by his misogyny: the male brain that continues to operate underneath layers of makeup and stolen feminine flesh.

Buffalo Bill is not the only individual undergoing transformation in this book. All the characters appear in a state of "becoming"; it is just that their transitions are less radical—more psychological than physiological—and viewed more positively by Harris. The death of his wife, Bella, has challenged Jack Crawford's personal outlook on the world; her loss has deeply affected the human being underneath the exterior of the Federal Bureau of Investigation bureaucrat. Hannibal Lecter deludes the authorities and escapes by wearing the face of the policeman he has just murdered. And he departs the novel about to undergo radical facial surgery to become someone else. In spite of his obsessive need to control the dynamics of their relationship, the doctor also seems to have been affected by his contact with Clarice Starling. In his final letter to her, he acknowledges the degree to which she has influenced him: "I have no plans to call on you, Clarice, the world being more interesting with you in it." [10]

His psychopathic cruelty notwithstanding, Lecter is Harris's most compelling character to date. He embodies what film theorist Robin Wood has labeled the "ambivalence of the horror Monster," at once "horrifying us with his evil and delighting us with his intellect, his art, his audacity; while our moral sense is appalled by his outrages, another part of us gleefully identifies with him." [11] Amoral and unemotional, Lecter is a pure intellect and consummate gamesplayer. But he is also intensely human—an empathic therapist as well as a brilliant scholar. His love of Bach and "a window with a view" begin to suggest the complexities of his nature. An angel with horns, the doctor fascinates us with his dualities: both a paragon of civilized man and a connoisseur of human flesh. Yet Lecter's cannibalism is never just about eating. As when Do-larhyde ingests Blake's watercolor, Lecter's selections in dining reveal the essence of his personality; for him, cannibalism is a means of ex-erting absolute domination over another person. Moreover, his worldly sophistication is present even in what he chooses to eat—only the organs that constitute the "sweet meats." Lecter's proclivity toward consuming human body parts also helps to explain his success as a psychoanalyst. His occupation employs a kind of psychic cannibalism in the transfer-ence of one individual's feelings, thoughts, and wishes to another. The psychiatrist is attracted to Starling because of her physical beauty, but he also comes to savor her for other reasons: Lecter wants the details of Starling's tragic adolescence so that he can digest her anguish and make it his own. Her personal pain—the screams of the lambs—becomes his pain, and this is why he dines on lamb chops after listening to Starling's narrative about the spring slaughtering. It is Starling's simultaneous vul-nerability and strength in the face of her lingering childhood memories that establishes whatever respect Lecter is capable of summoning toward another human being—particularly one he does not intend to eat.

Harris's novels, like the work of so many writers in the Gothic tradi-tion (from Mary Shelley to Stephen King) highlight the conflict between forces of rationality and human civilization and the irrational, destructive acts of individuals who have suffered severe rejection from the society they now seek to destroy symbolically. Certainly a main reason for Han-nibal Lecter's attractiveness to readers is that he fully embodies this dialectic within his own personality: the cannibal is never far removed from the scholar. Harris's "monsters" are social outcasts; similar to Mary Shelley's monster, Jame Gumb and Francis Dolarhyde were not born monsters, but were created by society's reductive definitions of gender, parenting, normalcy, and acceptability. Likewise, Lander and the mem-bers of the radical terrorist group in *Black Sunday* are the cyclical products of historical violence and political betrayals. For all these char-acters, rebellion against personal codes of conduct, gender definitions, political hegemony, and morality itself must be seen as the consequence of social repression and abuse.

These individuals are, on the other hand, out of control; their social torment has transformed them into society's torturers. Consequently, Harris's sympathy for their plights is necessarily limited. True to the detective genre that has influenced Harris as much as the Gothic, there is a need to control them and to reestablish some palpable order to coun-terbalance the terror Black September, Gumb, Dolarhyde, and Lecter

have unleashed upon the world. Harris's detectives—Major David Kaba-
kov, Will Graham, Jack Crawford, and Clarice Starling—are the heroes
and heroine of *Black Sunday*, *Red Dragon*, and *The Silence of the Lambs*,
respectively. They place themselves in opposition to the destruction and
madness that are the consequences of psychopathic behavior. Graham
and Starling, in particular, are compelled into bonding with the female
victims in *Red Dragon* and *The Silence of the Lambs*. These detectives are
committed to restoring the individuality and human dignity that Dolarhyde and Jame Gumb strip from their female victims in the
transformative process of objectifying all women into grandmother/
mother surrogates.

In spite of their unwavering dedication to an essentially moral vision
of life, Harris's detectives are nonetheless deeply shaken by their close
contact with evil. In *Red Dragon*, Graham often appears on the verge of
insanity. Lecter is acutely aware of Graham's susceptibility and enjoys
taunting him with this prospect. On several occasions, Dr. Lecter suggests an affinity between himself and the detective, and this parallel so
unnerves Graham that he must conscientiously work to repel its implications.[12] Only Graham's contact with his wife and stepchild separates him
from the realm of madness he is forced to endure each time he must
track severely disturbed men such as Lecter and Dolarhyde.

In *The Silence of the Lambs*, Clarice Starling has no family to counter-
balance her own descent into hell. Perhaps this initial vulnerability helps
to explain why she emerges as the individual most transformed by her
experiences. From the beginning of the book, we are made aware of
Clarice as a woman operating in a male domain. On her way to visit
Lecter in prison, she is verbally assaulted by insults from the male pris-
oners and by Dr. Chilton's patronizing commentary. As she approaches
Lecter's cell, she "knew her heels announced her."[13] Once she is in
front of the doctor, he proceeds to examine intimate facets of her person—from her choice of perfume to the quality of her handbag and
shoes. Why does Harris underscore so much gender consciousness so
early in the novel? Most obviously, because this is a book that will center, at least in part, around women—particularly those gender traits that
distinguish women from men. Perhaps more important, these opening
scenes call attention to Starling as a female, and do so in order to illustrate that women in this culture are subject to constant linguistic, as well
as physical, violations and intrusions by men. Moreover, if Starling
hopes to capture the man who preys on women, she must somehow
transform the daily anger and outrage she feels as a woman into some-

thing useful: "The proximity of madmen—the thought of Catherine Martin bound and alone, with one of them snuffling her, patting his pockets for his tools—braced Starling for her job. But she needed more than resolution. She needed to be calm, to be still, to be the keenest instrument. She had to use patience in the face of the awful need to hurry." [14]

Any discussion of *The Silence of the Lambs* must include at least a brief mention of the enormous popularity this book has garnered, especially in light of the successful film adaptation that won several Academy Awards. *The Silence of the Lambs* catapulted Thomas Harris into national prominence. Its mass appeal notwithstanding, several groups, most notably those objecting to the negative image of homosexuality (represented by the psychotic transsexual) and the graphic level of violence perpetuated against women, were very vocal in their protest against book and film. [15] Detective novelist Sara Paretsky, in an article written for the opinion-editorial section of the *New York Times*, expressed her dissatisfaction with both Harris's work and those women readers who tacitly support his portrayal of violence against women by purchasing his novel: "So why should I be surprised that women are paying to read about a man flaying women alive and stripping off their skins? Or a man releasing starving rats inside a woman's vagina? That's what we're doing. And we're doing it enough to make *The Silence of the Lambs* and *American Psycho* best sellers. . . . Why do women as well as men want to read about these exploits in vivid detail that seeks to re-create the pain and humiliation of the attack?" [16]

The Silence of the Lambs is much more than just another tale of misogyny and violent titillation. In fact, in the end it has more in common with the heroic quest—to create a world of greater security and beauty where women need not be afraid—than it does with the recreation of pain and humiliation. Paretsky ignores the major contribution Clarice Starling makes to this novel, thereby overlooking an answer to her own rhetorical questions: women readers are drawn to Harris's novel because they strongly identify with Starling. Indeed, she is ironically similar to Paretsky's own female detective—if not a sister of V. I. Warshawski, then at least a close cousin. Like Warshawski, Starling is a woman who does battle against the patriarchy, in all of its violent and oppressive manifestations, and the commitment to her (feminist) work is ultimately its own reward.

Starling is "toughened" by her contact with men. As a result, she comes to know the men in this book better than they—even the one who wishes to become female—ever learn to know women. And, of course, she is angered and frustrated by what she learns. Hannibal Lecter asks her, "how do you manage your rage?"—a question that becomes as important to Clarice as it is to the officious psychiatrist.[17] For the better part of the novel, Clarice is surrounded by men who either patronize women or murder them: Lecter, Buffalo Bill, Crawford, Chilton, and the male-dominated bureaucracy of the FBI itself (her status as a woman is underscored by her other "subordinate" role as student agent who must operate under the constant threat of being "recycled"). Without a conscious effort to exercise self-control and discipline, contact with these men and their patriarchal institutions might have produced a woman overwhelmed by her rage against male sexism and aggression. But this is not what happens. The importance of the final scene in the novel, curiously left undeveloped in the film version (where Starling shares a "deep and sweet" bed with the noble Pilcher), suggests that she certainly has not given in to the urge to reject males, or to place them into the sexist categories that the men in this book assign to her and the other women characters.

Harris's book is not only about the screaming of lambs; it is also about their silencing. Starling must somehow silence the anger she feels toward men. But the silence she finds does not come from repression, sublimation, or contribution to the madness by becoming a crazed anti-male revenger who seeks to punish men for their random carnage. Instead, Starling assumes control over her anger by pursuing what she can change—in herself as well as in the world. By focusing her emotions and energies, Buffalo Bill becomes a symbol for the perversity that men perpetuate upon women—behavior that Starling understands intimately and translates into an empathetic bond with Bill's female victims.

If *Red Dragon* operates in an essentially male-centered universe, *The Silence of the Lambs* is female-centered. The narrative action of *Red Dragon* is completely male-generated: the main characters are all men, while the novel's female characters appear as parallel models to Blake's feminine representation in his "Red Dragon" painting: terrified, supplicant, and victimized. *The Silence of the Lambs,* on the other hand, embodies an altogether different gender perspective; the women in this book are not isolated victims. In fact, they band together to fight both their isolation and victimization. Catherine Martin, the last intended addition to Gumb's collection, makes her own rescue possible because she actively helps herself. Instead of assuming the role of sacrificial lamb in his ritualized slaughter, Catherine's refusal to panic allows her to outwit

Gumb and gain more time. A similar level of inner strength characterizes Starling's roommate, Ardelia Mapp. While the latter does not participate in the direct action of the narrative, her presence subtly shapes the way Starling views other women—and eventually herself: "Of the two brightest people Starling knew, one [Mapp] was also the steadiest person she knew and the other [Lecter] was the most frightening. Starling hoped that gave her some balance in her acquaintance."[18] Clarice and Mapp share a noncompetitive, mutually respectful relationship that serves as a balance to counterpoint the fierce misogyny and spiritual anguish that threatens to engulf whatever is life affirming in this novel. In those moments when Starling is made to feel the weight of what appears to be a male collusion against her, Mapp offers crucial support and counsel.

As Starling learns to discipline herself, she comes to trust deeply in what is both scorned and coveted by the men in this book: her femininity. She tells Crawford that "The victims are all women and there aren't any women working on this. I can walk into a woman's room and know three times as much about her as a man would know."[19] It is the woman in Starling who makes the discovery of Buffalo Bill possible. Only a female would interest Lecter sufficiently to gain his trust and help. A female would be more likely to recognize the sewing link between Fredrica Bimmel and Gumb. And only another female would be capable of identifying so completely with Gumb's victims that she becomes as obsessed with his capture as he is with the skins of his captives. Starling translates feminist theory into reality, and does so without ever compromising her humanity.

Although Gumb believes that the resolution to his own inner warfare between masculine and feminine—what Carl Jung has called animus and anima—rests in completing his transformation into a woman, we have seen that his journey results not in psychic integration, but in its opposite—disintegration. Only Starling is able to integrate harmoniously the opposing parts of herself. To achieve this level of integration we must "become conscious that within ourselves we have combined opposites and need no longer project our personal devil onto others."[20] As he is intimately involved in uncovering her "personal devil" throughout the novel, Hannibal Lecter puts Starling into contact with her shadow—the "negative side of her personality."[21] He challenges Clarice to acknowledge her unconscious or repressed self and the unresolved hostility she still harbors toward her childhood: specifically her memory of abandonment and victimization symbolized in her identification with the endangered lambs and the horse, Hannah. Contact with the shadow instructs her in how to integrate the positive characteristic with the negative. As Neumann asserts, "Only by making friends with the shadow do we gain the friendship of Self."[22] Her remembered pain, which Lecter coerces her to reexamine, becomes a measure of Starling's capacity for constructive, righteous anger and the self-discipline necessary to survive in the present. In confronting her shadow by allowing Lecter to lead her back into the darkness of her childhood, Starling discovers the positive side of what the shadow proffers and integrates into her personality. As Jung describes the process, it is a considerable moral effort: "To become conscious of it [the shadow] involves recognizing the dark aspects of the personality. . . . This act is the essential condition for any kind of self-knowledge."[23] Starling is able to secure what Dolarhyde and Gumb passionately desire (yet never actually attain) from deep inside their respective gender hells: a resolution to the conflict between animus and anima that creates a psychic world of wholeness and maturation.

One of the great rewards in reading *The Silence of the Lambs* is savoring the complex set of relationships Starling establishes with Hannibal Lecter and Jack Crawford. While the two men appear to use Starling as a vehicle in their continuing mental warfare against each other, thereby deepening the novel's theme of women being exploited by men, they also occupy remarkably similar roles insofar as they emerge as competing father figures and teachers to Starling. Crawford instructs her about detective procedurals and, conversely, the importance of knowing when her instincts may be superior to "imposed patterns of symmetry."[24] Lecter, as I have already noted, is likewise interested in teaching Starling valuable information about the criminal psyche, but his approach is always more personal, and therefore perhaps more impressionable because it strikes to the essence of Starling's personality. In turn, Starling provides a certain measure of human dignity to Lecter, and this becomes partial explanation for his willingness to instruct her. Although the authorities acknowledge the power of his intellect and amoral will, their terror makes it impossible for them to appreciate his humanity; Lecter remains an exotic, albeit dangerous object to be studied and exploited. While Starling is always willing to exploit him, she also accords him a level of genuine respect that is, ironically, shared elsewhere only by Dolarhyde and Gumb. As Greg Garrett argues, "Whether unconsciously or consciously, Clarice, who knows what it's like to be an object, treats Lecter as human rather than object, and the lesson is not lost on him."[25] Starling needs both her mentors to advance—personally and professionally; through their inimitable pedagogies, they teach her the same thing: the value of balancing self-trust against self-restraint, and the importance of recognizing when to apply either.

Danse Macabre, Stephen King's analytical treatment of the Gothic genre in fiction and film, provides a useful theoretical paradigm for comprehending horror art. In particular works such as Harris's, which revolve around anomalous beings who are morally and ontologically transgressive, King notes: "The horror story, beneath its fangs and fright wig, is really as conservative as an Illinois Republican in a three-piece pinstriped suit; its main purpose is to reaffirm the virtues of the norm by showing us what awful things happen to people who venture into taboo lands. Within the framework of most horror tales we find a moral code so strong it would make a Puritan smile. . . . [T]he horror tale generally details the outbreak of some Dionysian madness in an Apollonian existence, and the horror will continue until the Dionysian forces have been repelled and the Apollonian norm restored again." [26] Noël Carroll takes King's thesis a step further when he argues that the horror tale ends with "the norm emerging stronger than before; it has been, so to say, tested; its superiority to the abnormal is vindicated." [27] This pattern of thematic and philosophical exposition is exactly what occurs in *Black Sunday*, *Red Dragon*, and *The Silence of the Lambs*. Only Hannibal Lecter's escape at the end of *The Silence of the Lambs* would appear to subvert this narrative design. His reemergence into the world tends to qualify the novel's concluding restoration of "the Apollonian norm" and proves, I suspect, that the very notion of a postmodern status quo is always an endangered concept.

The fictional transformations which are at the center of Thomas Harris's art all revolve around "ventures into taboo lands." The psychopathic criminals in his world want to enact some kind of radical transformation over society and/or themselves. For them, power is synonymous with domination and destruction. Against their Dionysian visions, Harris's detectives are poised in a counterstruggle of their own: how does one enter the world of madness—identifying with victim and murderer alike—apprehend a killer, and emerge with sanity and humanity intact? The transformative energies which stand in opposition to Harris's detectives, and to the readers who vicariously identify with them, are psychologically terrifying. The threats they represent are an assault on the basic assumptions of personal conduct and social interaction. Thus, the reader is manipulated subtly into sharing a level of investment in the conservative worldview that Harris summons to refute these threats; for as they are encoded within the contexts of his fiction, "the virtues of the norm" are inevitably reaffirmed with a sigh of relief.

Notes

I would like to thank the International Conference for the Fantastic in the Arts for permitting me the opportunity to read an abbreviated version of this chapter at their March 1994 meeting in Fort Lauderdale, Florida. I am also indebted to the following individuals for their ideas, advice, and inspiration: Brian Kent, Fred Frank, Sidney Poger, and Leonard Cassuto.

1. James Twitchell, *Dreadful Pleasures: An Anatomy of Modern Horror* (New York: Oxford University Press, 1985) 66.

2. Twitchell 241.

3. Thomas Harris, *Red Dragon* (New York: New American Library, 1981) 223–24.

4. Harris, *Red Dragon* 296.

5. Mario Praz, *The Romantic Agony* (New York: Oxford University Press, 1970) 21.

6. Alfred Kazin, *The Portable Blake* (New York: Viking, 1968) 21.

7. Harris, *Red Dragon* 96.

8. Mary Lynn Johnson, "Feminist Approaches to Teaching *Songs*," *Approaches to Teaching Blake's Songs of Innocence and of Experience*, eds. Robert F. Glecknew, and Mark L. Greenberg (New York: Modern Language Association, 1989) 61.

9. Thomas Harris, *The Silence of the Lambs* (New York: St. Martin's Press, 1988) 96.

10. Harris, *Silence* 337.

11. Robin Wood, *Hollywood from Vietnam to Reagan* (New York: Columbia University Press, 1986) 80.

12. Harris, *Red Dragon* 67–68.

13. Harris, *Silence* 12.

14. Harris, *Silence* 129.

15. See the post-Academy Award editorial entitled "Dark Victory" in *The Nation* (20 April 1992): 507–508, where *The Silence of the Lambs* is condemned as an amoral, politically incorrect film that "trumpets sadomasochism, homophobia, misogyny and worse" (507).

16. Sara Paretsky, "Soft Spot for Serial Murderers," *New York Times* 28 Apr. 1991, sec. 4, p17.

17. Harris, *Silence* 155.

18. Harris, *Silence* 252.

19. Harris, *Silence* 274.

20. Barbara Rogers-Gardner, *Jung and Shakespeare* (Wilmette: Chiron Publications, 1992) 39.

21. Carl G. Jung, "Aion: Phenomenology of the Self," in *The Portable Jung*, trans. R. F. C. Hull (New York: Viking, 1971) 147.

22. Erich Neumann, *The Origins and History of Consciousness*, trans. R. F. C. Hull (Princeton: Princeton University Press, 1970) 353.

23. Jung 145.

24. Harris, *Silence*, 70.

25. Greg Garrett, "Objecting to Objectification: Re-viewing the Feminine in *The Silence of the Lambs.*" *Journal of Popular Culture* 27 (1994): 1–12.

26. Stephen King, *Danse Macabre*, rev. ed. (New York: Berkeley, 1982) 368.

27. Noël Carroll, *The Philosophy of Horror, or Paradoxes of the Heart* (New York: Routledge, 1990) 201.

3

Stephen King's Canon
The Art of Balance

Edwin F. Casebeer

Stephen King is the most popular horror novelist today (and also the most popular novelist). He is the only writer ever to have made the Forbes 500; his annual income exceeds that of some third-world countries. His works are a significant percentage of the book industry's annual inventory. The average American recognizes his name and face. Yet, paradoxically, his novels also top the lists of censored authors. Perhaps that is because he creates fiction and cinema about that which we would rather avoid: modern meaninglessness, physical corruptibility, and death. Do the fictional situations he presents argue for a decline in our culture's energy for life, a descending depression and despair that lends enchantment to the graveyard, the kind of apocalyptic view that often ends centuries and heralds new human hells? Or is his appeal understandable in a way that affirms our culture and its willingness to deal with its dilemmas?

If we begin with Stephen King's status among his immediate peers—the horror novelists—the reasons for his broad appeal are clear. He has taken command of the field by writing representative masterworks: the vampire novel *('Salem's Lot)*, the monster novel *(The Dark Half)*, wild talent fiction *(Carrie)*, zombie fiction *(Pet Sematary)*, diabolic possession fiction *(Christine)*, and realistic horror fiction *(Misery)*. His presence in the field extends to its very boundaries.

But King is actually a genre novelist; that is, he writes in all of the major popular genres now marketed to the country's largest reading population: horror, fantasy, science fiction, the western, the mystery, and the romance. While he works in pure forms *('Salem's Lot* as a vampire novel, *Cycle of the Werewolf* as a werewolf novel, *The Talisman* as a quest fantasy, and *The Running Man* as science fiction), he often mixes genres. An early example is *The Stand,* particularly its first published edition, which begins as one form of the science fiction novel (the apocalyptic), evolves into a second form (the utopian), and concludes as a fantasy which blends elements of the quest like Tolkien's *Lord of the Rings* trilogy with Christian apocalyptic fantasy like *The Omen* trilogy.[1] Similarly, his *Dark Tower* trilogy combines apocalyptic science fiction with Arthurian quest fantasy, itself subordinated to the western, and then introduces science fiction's alternate worlds concept. The standard detective mystery does much to shape *The Dark Half, Needful Things,* and *Dolores Claiborne,* while the Gothic romance and the feminist novel are essential features of *Misery, Gerald's Game,* and *Dolores Claiborne.* The resulting breadth gives his fiction a much wider appeal than might come to a "pure" horror writer.

But King's appeal is even broader than that of a genre writer. From the beginning of his career, he was responsive to those horror writers of his decade, like Ira Levin, who moved from the traditional confines of the *fantastique* to establish analogies between the world that we all occupy and the horror novel's traditional settings, situations, plots, and characters. King, too, grounds fantasy in realism. In fact, his earliest published work, *Rage* (published under the Richard Bachman pseudonym), is a capable realistic novel. Motivated by his own boyhood and his involvement with his children, King's early novels demonstrate strong characterizations of preadolescent boys and small children. In the ensuing years, he has added to his palette, and now is taking up the challenge of realistic female protagonists.

King's appeal thus broadens even further: this realism opens up a subtext that addresses urgent contemporary concerns. From his youth, he has been a man of his generation; a man with deep political awareness and involvement. As has been elaborated critically by such works as Tony Magistrale's *Landscape of Fear* and Douglas Winter's *The Art of Darkness,* King has created many novels which allegorically address current social dilemmas: the corruption of school and church *(Rage, Carrie, Christine),* the government *(The Long Walk, Firestarter, The Running Man, The Stand, The Dead Zone),* the small town *('Salem's Lot, It, Needful Things, Tommyknockers),* the family *(The Shining, Cujo, It, Christine),* and heterosexual relationships *(Gerald's Game, Dolores Claiborne).* Thus, King's work offers more than mere escape fiction or "adrenaline" fiction; it urges readers to confront squarely and disturbingly the horror in their own lives. The resulting depth connects him to an audience drawn to literature more "serious" than horror or genre fiction. His model has inspired enough followers to cause horror fiction to move to the front of bookstores and the top of the *New York Times'* bestseller list. It is not so much that the reading public has developed a perverse taste for horror as it is that, emulating King, horror writers have broadened and deepened their art enough to address us all on issues of consequence.

Paramount among these issues is death. As James Hillman pointed out in *Revisioning Psychology,* contemporary Western culture is the first extensive culture which has had to consider death as an ending, rather than as a transformation. Instead of believing in a transformation into an angel or devil, animal, or star, today's rationalists regard being as matter and unanimated being as refuse. Founded upon such materialism, the contemporary state and school have reinterpreted reality so as to provide for the here and now, and have maintained a polite skepticism about other realities. King repeatedly dramatizes, from an evolving perspective, the dilemma in which we find ourselves: we are without resources before the imminence of our own deaths and the catastrophe of the deaths of those we love. Adopting (such as in *Carrie*) a contemporary existentialist attitude (where the only constants are isolation, decay, and death), King explores such values (acts, creations, children) as may survive death or those entertained by other cultures (as in *The Stand*). In other novels (such as *The Talisman* and *The Dark Tower* series) King will entertain the possibilities suggested by post-Einsteinian physicists (the multiverse, the reality of process and the nonexistence of time, space, and matter). As in *It,* King looks at possibilities suggested by the psychoanalytic architects of reality, particularly the Jungian theory of an archetypal dimension underlying matter—a dimension that can be apprehended and molded by the artistic imagination. Although King sometimes ends his novels in nausea *(Pet Sematary)* or nothingness *(Carrie),* normally he views the human condition in terms of possibilities and affirmations. Again representative of his generation—and his American community (small-town New England)—those affirmations are based upon what is possible for the individual, particularly the individual not blinded by rationalism. He displays deep distrust for any human configuration larger than the family.

Although King's thematic reach is wide and deep, ascertaining his position on any given issue is not simple. This ambiguity also underlies his broad appeal, for vastly different readers may arrive at vastly different conclusions about his agenda. King seems, in a novel like *The Stand,* to be able to appreciate the validity of the opposed positions of a small-town Christian, Republican American with a high school education and a sophisticated, liberal, and urban existentialist. In a way, like Shakespeare, he does not conclusively resolve a plot or commit irrevocably to the agenda of a specific character or group of characters involved in the conflict. But his noncommitment is so submerged that readers normally assume (as they have with Shakespeare for centuries) that he agrees with them; he economically gestures toward the possibility of gestalt, not a specific gestalt. On the contrary, his chief artistic talent—the talent that has kept all of his work in print throughout his career and is likely to keep it in print—is his ability to balance opposing realities. The reader must resolve the issues. If we supinely regard King as simply a popular artist and expect a canned resolution, we often will find his resolutions unsatisfying. If we invest the energy in tipping his balance toward ourselves, we will behold in the artistic experience an affirming and illuminating mirror of our problems and our solutions.

Such a mirror develops not only from King's choice of situations of great concern to us, but by his technique of characterization. Here again, he achieves balance, gains breadth and depth of appeal. In one sense, King is a highly accomplished realist with a keen eye for the nuances of image and voice; but, in another, his characters are archetypal with origins in myth and folktale. Characters fall into two large groups—the sketch and the multidimensional. One of his true talents is the sketch: he is able to populate novels like *'Salem's Lot*, *The Stand*, and *The Tommyknockers* with hundreds of briefly executed, vivid characters—each efficiently caught in a telling and representative moment that is often grotesque and generally memorable. King can make credible, as in *The Stand*, a plot that quite literally involves a whole country. He sketches characters from the South, New York, New England, the West, from the rural and urban blue-collar class, the middle class, the criminal and indigent, the police, the army, the entertainment world, and the clerks and functionaries of cities and small towns from all over America. These characters, placed in highly detailed topographies, create for us the realistic element of his fantasies so central in enabling us to accept their supernatural premises. As King said in an interview with Magistrale: "The work underlines again and again that I am not merely dealing with the surreal and the fantastic but, more important, using the surreal and the fantastic to examine the motivations of people and the society and the institutions they create." [2]

King's realistic techniques for creating the primary multidimensional characters significantly differs from those producing the sketch. Gener-

ally speaking, he avoids the customary expository visual portrait of a
primary character; he prefers to develop the character internally. Thus,
by beginning in the character's sensorium, we can project more quickly
and directly into it than we might if the objectification of a physical
description was between us and it: existing as the bound Jessie Burlingame in *Gerald's Game*, we see, hear, touch, taste, and smell her
experience of her world; and from these physical experiences we enter
into and share her psychological presence. Generally, we find that psychological presence to be archetypal—the anima. Like any popular artist
working with the stereotypical, King is always on the border of creating
Jungian personae and plots emanating from the cultural unconscious.
Therefore, however individually a multidimensional character may be
textured, it feels very familiar as we settle into it.

But King goes a step further, particularly in his more epic novels,
by exemplifying the theories of such neo-Jungian thinkers as Hillman:
(1) the human psyche is basically a location for a cast of personae in
dynamic relationship with one another; (2) the one-persona psyche—
humanity's current and dominant commitment to unity, integration, and
control—is pathological (the excesses of the rationalistic materialist); and
(3) the universe and its inhabitants can only be seen clearly through
multiple and dynamic perspectives.[3] Thus, except in novellas and short
stories, King generally prefers multiple points of view. Here he is influenced by modernists (such as Faulkner) and by cinema: perspective
follows setting—and if the setting contains different characters, he still
develops multiple points of view. In the larger novels, typically King
pits a group of comrades against a common threat, a dynamic for which
he found precedent in both Tolkien's *The Ring* trilogy and Stoker's *Dracula*.[4] Though the details produced by setting and sensorium conceal the
fact, each comrade is a persona—a specialized and archetypal figure such
as the child, the old man, the lover, the teacher, the healer, etc. As the
plot progresses and each persona contributes its vision, the remaining
personae subsume these perspectives and evolve into a single (hero or
heroine) or dyadic (lovers or parent/child) protagonist with the capacity
to defeat or stalemate the antagonist, which itself is often a persona
embodying death, decay, or meaninglessness.

Just as often, however, the antagonist is the monstrous. King has a
particularly complex attitude toward such a persona. Like Clive Barker,
King is able to see the positive side of the monstrous—its incredible
energy and commitment, its individuality, and its ability to function in
the unknown. Unlike Barker, he is not ready to embrace the monstrous

and let it transform him. Again, balance prevails. In *Danse Macabre*, King analyzes the function of author and antagonist in novels. For him, the authorial is not the autobiographical; the "King" is another persona—the folksy, small-town Maine citizen of the commercials, of the prefaces, and of the authorial asides. The persona of the author agrees with the norms of the community.[5] But the antagonist (as monster) is that shadow aspect of us which finds its reality in the individual, the bizarre, and the grotesque. This antagonist seeks to tyrannically control or to destroy rather than to belong, which is dynamic rather than centered and driven rather than ordered. We contain both and we come to the novel to experience both. Their conflict will never be settled, for it is the essence of what they are: opposites that define one another. Although Thad Beaumont, the protagonist of *The Dark Half*, wins his conflict with George Stark (the monster within him) we learn in *Needful Things* that he has lost his love, his art, and his family—he has settled back into alcoholism. In summary, the traditional horror novel, such as Bram Stoker's *Dracula*, excises or conquers the antagonist; the postmodernist horror novel, such as Clive Barker's works, transforms the protagonist into the antagonist, or vice versa; and King's novels balance these processes.

The end result of such a dynamic perception of character and structure is that the novel becomes psyche: that is, it is the location of archetypal personae and their dynamics. It is the interface between the psyches of writer and reader, a template of the soul, a mirror in which we see ourselves most clearly in terrain we least care to explore, the nightworld of death and monstrosity. Seen from the above perspectives, King becomes a modern shaman employing magic (the fantasy image, childhood imagination) to lead his culture into self-discovery where it most needs to look while maintaining commitment to love, family, and community—for King is also a husband, father, and highly visible "social" presence. Again he balances: he is of the tribe and he directs the tribe. No wonder we read him; no wonder we approach him with caution.

Because of his inclination to balance consecutive novels by opposing them to one another, these propositions apply more to the broad characteristics and processes of the canon rather than to individual novels. But his novels also fall into categories in which the same striving toward the balancing of opposing forces is evident: the community, the child, the writer, the woman, and the quest. These categories not only provide a more useful way of approaching King's fiction specifically than would a chronological or genre discussion, but they also focus the preceding theoretical discussion. Each category is a broad, shared foundation with the reader upon which and through which King can consistently design and redesign his social allegories and the psyche's archetypal templates that so consistently and profoundly link him with his audience.

King's writings about the community establish him as one of the country's major regionalist writers whose influences can be traced to the New England Gothic writers, Thornton Wilder's *Our Town*, and the novels of William Faulkner. The community which King most often chooses to present is one inspired by the town of his childhood—Durham, Maine.[6] Sometimes the town is Jerusalem's Lot of the *'Salem's Lot* stories, Haven of *The Tommyknockers*, or Castle Rock—the setting of such works as "The Body," *Cujo, The Dead Zone, The Dark Half,* and *Needful Things*. A citizen of his region, King believes that the most politically viable unit is one small enough to hear and respond to individual opinion; as in *The Stand*, cities like New York regularly appear in an advanced state of disruption and the federal government responds only to the reality of its paper and its power.

Although community is more feasible in a small town than in a large city, in King's small towns it is rare. More frequently, their citizens (as in *'Salem's Lot, The Tommyknockers*, and *Needful Things*) are caught up in materialistic pursuits that lead them into conflict with their neighbors. This conflict results in a community held together by conformity rather than cooperation, with narcissism and the closed door, fealty to no code but self-gratification, and apocalypse simmering beneath the surface. Yet—to stress King's seeking of balance in this category—there appears the option of a better way of life. The Boulder Free Zone of *The Stand* comes closest to such a utopia: it is small, it accords a place to each according to need and talent, and it attends to the individual. But King is ambivalent about such a grassroots democracy; the true reason for the survival of the Free Zone is the emergence of an elite presiding coterie composed of exceptional individuals with exceptional social conscience. When events demand the sacrifice of most of these people and the Free Zone becomes too large for rule by their dialogue, Stu Redman and Fran Goldsmith (the surviving hero and heroine) conclude that their community now is simply recycling the former decadent and materialist world. They opt for a more viable social unit: the family. And they leave the Free Zone for the locale of King's own family, Maine.

To understand King's strong focus on the family and the child requires recognition that during his career he has been a husband and father of two boys and a girl. During their childhood, he generally worked at home, but brought his family with him on the rare occasions when he left Maine.[7] Thus, his family is often major material; he need only look up from the word processor to find grist. And as his own children have aged, so has the presence of the child diminished in his novels. The category of the child arises for a second reason: in his own development, King has had to reencounter himself as child and boy in order to remove the blocks to his becoming a man: "The idea is to go back and confront your childhood, in a sense relive it if you can, so that you can be whole."[8] Also in this category are early novels such as *Rage* (begun while he was in high school), *The Long Walk*, and *Carrie* (written by a young man dealing with problems posed by family and organized adult society).

Among King's most endearing characters are small children such as Danny Torrance of *The Shining* and Charlie McGee of *Firestarter*. In their characterization, he avoids the potential sentimentality that often sinks such efforts by manipulating sentences that seamlessly weave together the diction and phrasing of both child and adult, thus conveying the being of the one and the perspective of the other. The second paragraph introducing Danny provides an example: "Now it was five o'clock, and although he didn't have a watch and couldn't tell time too well anyway, he was aware of passing time by the lengthening of the shadows, and by the golden cast that now tinged the afternoon light."[9] The first subordinate clause is childishly run-on in structure and uses Danny's diction, while the second main clause is complex-compound within itself—its subordinate elements are parallel and its diction is the polysyllabic format typical of the narrator in King's lyric mode. Such a combination of styles and perspectives works so well because King adheres to the romantic belief that the child is the father of the man. It may be that children are superior in wisdom and psychological talents to adults simply because the latter are corrupted by psyches shrunken by materialism and rationalism—but they are superior. Thus, Danny is one with time and space, almost godlike in his perception of those dimensions in the haunted Hotel Overlook, while Charlie's power over the material world establishes her as an angel of apocalypse when she incinerates the Shop (King's version of the CIA).

King's adolescents can also be superior to his adults. In fact, the major reason for grouping the adolescent with the child is that, normally, King's adolescents are prepubescent: they have no explicit sexual identity and are still more child than adult. It is in such adolescents that we see his attempt to achieve yet another kind of balance—between the two stages of life. While the child has intimations of immortality, the adult has knowledge of death. Thus, the Castle Rock novella "The Body" (made into the excellent film by Rob Reiner entitled *Stand By Me*) initiates its four boys by leading them not into a sexual encounter, but into another rite of passage: their first encounter with death as the corpse of a fifth boy. Similarly, in *It*, a group of boys encounters and prevails over the protean incarnation of every human's deepest fear; and in *The Talisman*, co-written with Peter Straub, a trio of boys (an archetypal id, ego, and superego) transcend the force of this reality to enter a reality in which death is unempowered. Sometimes, as in *Carrie, The Stand*, and *Christine*, death and sexuality are negatively related: as Carrie becomes sexual, she becomes monstrous and an angel of the apocalypse. The sexual foreplay of Nadine and Harold in *The Stand* is a clear symptom of their degenerate state. As Arnie becomes sexual, Christine corrupts him—even Arnie's benevolent alter ego, Dennis, discovers that his first love turns to ashes. In his most recent novels, King demonstrates a mature and central sexuality; but in the novels of this earlier period, in which he is reencountering his boyhood, sexuality leads to adulthood which leads to diminished psychological resources and death.

Coincidental with King's emphasis on the child and the boy is his emphasis on the family (often in a pathological phase). One of the earliest and most powerful of these novels is *The Shining*, which, long before systems theory, dramatized the point that the pathological individual is a symptom of the pathological family and that both must undergo treatment. Jack Torrance's obsessions and his wife's posture as victim are inheritances from their parents which bind them together and threaten Danny. In *Christine*, Arnie's pathological family environment leads to his destruction and theirs, while Dennis's family supports and creates him in its image. *It* provides the reader with a wide range of family dynamics, both successful and unsuccessful, and relates such to the girl and boys who are the protagonists. The most powerful of the numerous family novels is the tragic *Pet Sematary*, which develops for the reader a realistically ideal family which is demolished by its own estimable values when its child is senselessly killed. The question posed by the novel is whether the family can survive the death of a child. The answer is no. In this system, the death of a child kills the family.

A subject as close to King as the child and the family is that of the writer—a character who dominates as either protagonist or antagonist in a wide range of short stories, novellas, and novels (most significantly *'Salem's Lot, The Shining, It, Misery, The Tommyknockers,* and *The Dark*

Half). The novelist-protagonist who dominates *'Salem's Lot* is more a product of King's youthful ideals than his experience. Like King, Ben Mears (a "mirror") undertakes a novel which will allow him to productively relive his childhood. But Ben's conflict with the vampire Barlow enlarges him to mythic proportions: as the personae about him converge and provide him understanding, faith, wisdom, and imagination, he develops a godlike perception and power. Metaphorically, when he encounters and conquers the vampire that is feeding on the town, he becomes the archetype of an elemental "good . . . whatever moved the greatest wheels of the universe."[10] The following novel, *The Shining*, establishes balance by becoming an exact opposite to its predecessor: the alcoholic Torrance (a playwright this time) is the monster. King sees this particular writer as a failure because he stops writing—Torrance's writing block leads to psychosis. Among the complex communities of *The Stand*, a similar opposition is in the contrast between Larry (the successful musician) with Harold (the unsuccessful writer): although his success nearly destroys him, Larry literally enacts a second crucifixion that saves the world; abnegating art for dark vision, Harold still manages some dignity before succumbing to demonic forces. Both figures physically resemble King: Larry has King's height and current physique and Harold has the height and King's adolescent physique. Although the hero is blond and the villain dark-haired, both have hair the quality of King's. In *It*, where the child's imagination is the only weapon of the adult against the death and meaninglessness of the eponymous evil, the novelist Bill Denbrough (who this time resembles Peter Straub) regains this state most easily and thus is a vital element of the protagonistic band.

Balancing again, King writes two novels—*Misery* and *The Tommyknockers*—which countervail such optimistic authorial characterizations. In *Misery* the primary subject is the negative relationship of the reader and the writer: the reader is the writer's enemy. Readers regularly read the genre writer rather than the literary artist—in *Misery*, this is the Gothic novelist. Since the readers' choice enforces conventions and confines the writer's creative talent, in a sense the audience "writes" the genre novel. Apparently tiring of these limitations, King personifies his tyrannical audience in the archetypal figure of Annie, who literally limits the aspiring literary artist, Paul Sheldon, to genre fiction by drugs, bondage, and torture. Despite such a negative response to whether readers are the motivation for writing, King gives the issue a serious and detailed treatment: his writing of a Gothic romance novel within a realistic novel and his exploration of the psychological processes of writers and their relationship with those of readers is a fascinating and original effort. And, again, he negates his own negation by undercutting Paul's distaste for genre fiction by his admiration for this bloodily extracted romance, even though its creation mutilated him.

While *Misery* suggests that the literary artist's social influence is more negligible than that of a genre novelist by creating a character with a conflicting literary agenda, *The Tommyknockers* approaches the same issue by creating two authors: (1) the genre novelist, Bobbi Anderson, whose dark vision unleashes an alien presence which enslaves her community; and (2) the literary artist, poet Jim Gardener, whose self-sacrifice saves that community. Both are competent and dedicated writers who hold one another's work in esteem. But both are fatally flawed. Bobbi's kind of writing leaves her psychologically open to outside control (from audience and alien): she becomes the conduit which unearths and directs a cosmic darkness to the human community. Jim is armed against such possession, but isolated from the community by an art aspiring to the ideal. He has the vision to see through the darkness—he can and does die for the community, but it will never buy his books. As in *Misery*, King's final position on the writer's value is extremely pessimistic.

After writing *Misery* and *The Tommyknockers*, King entered a hiatus.[11] For him, writing had become an existential act. He had the money but he felt controlled and depleted by the audience that he did have and despaired of the existence of any other kind of audience. Why continue to write? Developmental theory, such as Gail Sheehy's *Passages*, suggests that other processes were affecting King. He was passing through a chronological period from the age of 38 to 42 in which a man or woman working in the public area generally experiences extreme conflict as life takes a new direction: he or she reaches the end of a horizontal direction in which new territory and material are claimed through a process of conflict (a masculine direction), and a vertical direction where depth rather than width is sought through the development of nurturance and personal relationships (a feminine direction).[12]

King emerged from his hiatus with an ambitious contract for four books—he wrote five (the last two of which were novels solely about women). But before he undertook this feminine direction, he closed the canon to children, Castle Rock, and writers. Children had by this time become lesser characters. The people of Castle Rock, given a slight nudge by a minor demon, destroyed themselves in the apocalyptic cataclysm ending *Needful Things*. The resolution of the issue of the writer in

The Dark Half was more complex. The opposition of popular writer and artist in *Misery* and *The Tommyknockers* is here internalized in *The Dark Half:* warring for the soul of a writer are his personae as literary artist (Thad Beaumont) and as genre novelist (George Stark). The artist wins, but the victory is pyrrhic. Closer examination reveals that Beaumont's friends, wife, and children are psychologically akin to his nemesis. We find out in the sequel, *Needful Things,* that not only has the artist lost friends and family, but also the will to write. He is an alcoholic and the circle is closed. King leaves the issue behind him unresolved: it is what it is.

In *Gerald's Game* and *Dolores Claiborne,* King picks up a gauntlet. Long criticized for unidimensional female characters in such articles as Mary Pharr's "Partners in the *Danse:* Women in Stephen King's Fiction," [13] he apparently decided that a new direction for growth both as human and as artist would be appropriate in accepting the challenge to create convincing women. Written simultaneously, the novels are most productively regarded as two poles in a meta-narrative process. At the one pole is the heroine of *Gerald,* Jessie Burlingame—economically and socially privileged, childless, and in her own eyes significant only as her husband's sexual object. At the other pole is Dolores, a figure apparently based on King's mother (to whom he dedicates the novel)—economically and socially underprivileged, a mother, and in her own eyes significant in herself. Through their telepathic awareness of one another and through their experience of the same eclipse as a central incident in their lives, King establishes the commonality of these two very different women: it lies in the fact that they are whole only in those years before and after men entered their lives—the period of the eclipse. In *Gerald,* King dramatizes the entry of Jessie into an eclipse through the seduction and domination by her father; she exits the eclipse by killing her dominating husband, Gerald. The subsequent fragmenting of her victim persona into a community of sustaining female personae provides her with the resources to free herself from a literal bondage. In *Dolores,* the titular figure is a mother and wife who exits the eclipse by murdering a husband who also seeks to sexually exploit his daughter. In either case, the women experience one horror in common: the entry of men and sexuality into their lives. By erecting such contrasting poles as Jessie and Dolores, and yet maintaining both as sympathetic characters with a shared dilemma, King writes paired novels sympathetic to a wide spectrum of women and evades an easy condemnation of his women characters as unidimensional.

Overall, King's canon is a quest. But his battle cry is not "excelsior!" The direction is downwards and the path is a spiral. Many of King's characters experience life as a quest: Ben Mears of *'Salem's Lot* questing for self and conquering the vampire; *The Tommyknockers'* Gardener questing for death and finding self; the comrades of *The Stand* marching against the Dark One and founding the New Jerusalem; the boys of *It* killing fear; and the boys of *The Talisman* killing death. The gunslinger of *The Dark Tower* series is, however, probably most typical of King: he seeks to understand what the quest itself is. His enemies become his friends, his guides his traitors, his victims those he has saved, and his now a then. Paradox; transformation; balancing the dualities, an emergent, tenuous, ever-fading, and ever-appearing balance—these are the duplicitous landmarks in the terrain of King's work and his life. Both are open enough and fluent enough to mirror us and ours as we seek to make our own accommodations with modern monsters, personal meaninglessness, social chaos, physical decay, and death.

Notes

1. Edwin F. Casebeer, "The Three Genres of *The Stand*," *The Dark Descent: Essays Defining Stephen King's Horrorscape*, ed. Tony Magistrale (Westport, Conn.: Greenwood Press, 1992) 47–59.

2. Tony Magistrale, *Stephen King: The Second Decade*, Danse Macabre *to* The Dark Half. (New York: Twayne, 1992) 15.

3. James Hillman, *Revisioning Psychology* (New York: Harper & Row, 1975) chap. 1.

4. Douglas E. Winter, *Stephen King: The Art of Darkness* (New York: Signet, 1986) 41, 61–62.

5. Stephen King, *Danse Macabre* (New York: Berkeley, 1982) 58.

6. George Beahm, *The Stephen King Story: A Literary Profile* (Kansas City: Andrews & McMeel, 1991) 27–29.

7. Winter 50.

8. Winter 185.

9. Stephen King, *The Shining* (New York: Signet, 1978) 26.

10. Stephen King, *'Salem's Lot* (New York: Signet, 1976) 408.

11. Stephen King, *Four Past Midnight* (New York: Viking, 1990) xv.

12. Gail Sheehy, *Passages* (New York: Dutton, 1976) 38–42.

13. Mary Pharr, "Partners in the *Danse:* Women in Stephen King's Fiction," *Dark Descent: Essays Defining Stephen King's Horrorscape*, ed. Tony Magistrale (New York: Greenwood Press, 1992) 19–32.

4

Living with(out) Boundaries
The Novels of Anne Rice

Lynda Haas and Robert Haas

"I want a lot. I want to be immortal."
—Anne Rice, Bill Moyers's interview

"Read between the lines."
—*The Vampire Lestat*

Castrated opera singers. Spirits who desire fleshly existence. Vampires and witches. The *gens de couleur*. Mummies who become immortal. These are the characters who occupy the margins of Anne Rice's fictional worlds. Boundary creatures, all. In her narratives that span time from the first recorded literate culture—the Sumerians who told the tale of Gilgamesh—to the present-day bustling with computers and fax machines, Rice always chooses to write about fugitives and nomads. And whether they are human or supernatural, they are characters who can never be part of the normal or dominant society. Between the lines of their narratives, Western society reads about itself and its own philosophical and physical struggles to place itself within cultural boundaries. This sympathy of the marginalized, perhaps, is why so many readers are drawn to the fictional worlds of Anne Rice. Even beyond the boundaries of her American audience, Rice's characters have become known to readers of the Gothic in several cultures.[1]

Although Rice has an increasing number of fans worldwide (and also some critical admirers), reviews of her work are usually filled with complaints that her writing is fetid, humid, overstuffed, baroque, pretentious, formulaic, and downright awful.[2] By new critical standards, perhaps Rice's novels do not have what it takes to "stand the test of time." Her novels are, however, interesting and important as cultural commentary, and as an intriguing combination of Gothic literary conventions with a postmodern sensibility about identity formation, sensual/sexual embodiment, and historical perspective. Whether she is writing about Louis or Lestat *(The Vampire Chronicles)*, Ramses *(The Mummy)*, or Rowan and Lasher (the *Taltos* series), the struggle of Rice's characters to understand shifting cultural boundaries becomes a means of interrogating who we are and how we live—questions with no easy answers.

Additionally, there is no contemporary writer with stronger ties to the Gothic tradition than Anne Rice. Beginning in 1976 with *Interview with the Vampire* and continuing to *Taltos*, Rice has consistently and successfully combined many of the Gothic conventions initiated by Horace Walpole in *The Castle of Otranto* (1763) with her own unique style and with the concerns of postmodern philosophy.[3] It is an enticing combination—a "witches' brew" of elements that millions of readers find difficult to resist. This essay concentrates on two texts, *The Vampire Lestat* and *The Mummy*, that include the supernatural. In addition, this essay analyzes postmodern elements of history and identity within all of Rice's novels and develops connections between these two contemporary issues and the Gothic tradition which spans two centuries.

History and Perspective

"We are miracles or horrors, depending on how you wish to see us."
—Armand

Since the arrival of "new historicism" (a postmodern approach to examining narratives), the act of writing and interpreting history has been problematic for its parallel to creating fiction. From Plutarch's account of Roman history and Holinshed's chronicles of England to Ken Burns's documentary of the Civil War and E. L. Doctorow's ficto-historical worlds, writers have exercised the literary license of describing historical persons, incidents, and places in a subjective way that meets their own narrational and ideological purposes. Rice's novels are often described as historical, for she uses well-known fragments of history as she traces her stories throughout various epochs; often interweaving and rewriting narratives familiar to the reader, Rice retells them in such a way as to open new interpretations. Her historical revisioning is so often tied to religious perspective that one might hypothesize her purpose in revising is to interrogate and replace the influences of the Christian era with influences that are decidedly pre- or post-Christian.

The use of history within narratives has always been an integral part of the Gothic tradition. Dracula's relationship to Genghis Khan or the ancient and exotic horrors of *Vathek* and *The Monk* rely on both natural and mythical history to advance the plot. These narratives' historical moments are related from a religious and highly moralistic perspective; conversely, Rice's approach to the historical conventions of the Gothic tradition is decidedly post-Christian. Specifically, Rice questions the validity of history and also removes the influence of Christian morality and its judgmental interpretation of historical figures and incidents that have greatly colored not only narratives, but culture and society in general.

In her 1989 novel, *The Mummy*, Ramses (a ficto-historical character himself—Ramses II of Egypt), the protagonist who has transcended death and walked the earth since the times of ancient Egypt, has an extended conversation with his twentieth-century counterparts in the novel. They offer their interpretations of history from ancient times to the industrial revolution; Ramses's perspectives—those of an ancient, pre-Christian king of Egypt—are quite different. Rice thus creates what could never exist outside the realm of fiction: a person who is from another time and place, but who now exists in the modern era. From his interpretations, the way he walks, the values he holds, and the way he reacts to the modern world around him, we are presented with a different kind of historical glimpse into the ancient past—one that historians cannot offer, but one that is presented within this fictional world as being every bit as historical as something in a textbook. Rice's narrative shows Ramses's perspective as having more information and as being untainted by later developments in Western culture.

To teach Ramses about history, Julie takes him to a twentieth-century diorama: Madame Tussaud's Wax Museum. He does not react well to the figures because he knew them when they were alive: "Cleopatra had been no Roman. Cleopatra had been a Greek and an Egyptian. And the horror was, Cleopatra meant something to these modern people of the twentieth century which was altogether wrong. She had become a symbol of licentiousness, when in fact she had possessed a multitude of amazing talents. They had punished her for her one flaw by forgetting everything else."[4] Although Ramses has much to offer the early twentieth-century characters in the way of opening up the limitations of their particular perspective, he also gains knowledge of the boundaries of his own standpoint as he notices that what has survived in the modern culture is not his perspective, but the Christian appropriation of Rome's culture, values, and perspectives: "Roman numerals. Everywhere he looked he saw them; on cornerstones, in the pages of books; on the facades of buildings. In fact, the art, the language, the spirit of Rome ran through this entire culture, hooking it firmly to the past. Even the concept of justice . . . had come down not from the barbarians who once ruled this place with their crude ideas of revealed law and tribal vengeance, but from the courts and judges of Rome where reason had reigned."[5]

As Rice's narrators question historical perspectives, she simultaneously interrogates cultural memory and how it, like identity, is constructed by language and ideology. When Ramses is first awakened (after having become tired of the world and sleeping through many centuries), he does not have his full memory—he regains it in flashes. The ways in which his memory is different than the memories inscribed by historians is often his starting point as he attempts to outline his narrative of history as a correction to what the twentieth century had forgotten. But then, to Ramses, Karl Marx and his philosophy are nothing more than "sheer nonsense, as far as he could see. A rich man, it seemed, writing about poor men when he did not know how their minds worked."[6] The work of Marx, so influential to anything that followed his moment in history, means nothing to Ramses. In the advantages and disadvantages of each particular perspective, Rice shows that history and memory, in all their different versions, are not foundations, but fragments dependent upon the culture and language from which they come.

In *The Mummy*, history, cultural perspective, and language are interconnected. Ramses must learn new languages in order to communicate, which allows Rice to comment on the role of language in culture from a postmodern perspective. Ramses explains: "Language is names, Julie. Names for people, objects, what we feel." He evaluates English as "a good language for thinking. Greek and Latin had been excellent for thinking. Egyptian, no. With each new language he had learned in his earlier existence his capacity for understanding had improved. Language made possible whole kinds of thinking."[7] The idea that language facilitates human thought and not that human thought facilitates language (in other words, the concept that everything is discursive in some way) is a philosophical tenet that emerged in the shift from structuralism to poststructuralism. This movement, a type of poststructural semiotics that examines both language and thought, has influenced many of the arts. Not until Rice (with perhaps the exception of English horror writer,

Clive Barker), though, has the movement infiltrated the mainstream of Gothic/horror fiction. Elliot responds to Ramses that "surely the ideas came first and then the language to express them," and Ramses answers that "even in Italy itself where the tongue [Latin] was born, the language made possible the evolution of ideas which would have been impossible otherwise." [8]

In *The Vampire Chronicles*, Rice introduces historical and cultural perspectives through the time in which each character is reborn or made as a vampire. The culture from which the characters originally come partially shapes their identity and philosophical perspective; for instance, Lestat is from the eighteenth-century "Age of Reason"—a time when "white-wigged Parisians tiptoed around in high-heeled satin slippers, pinched snuff, and dabbed at their noses with embroidered handkerchiefs" while "the poor hovered in doorways, shivering and hungry, and the crooked unpaved streets were thick with filthy slush." [9] Louis, however, was made during the romanticism of the nineteenth century. Both are marked by the dominant philosophical schools and ethical mores of their original culture. Even older is Armand, a sixteenth-century Renaissance vampire, who looks like a daVinci saint or "the little god from Caravaggio." [10] Armand's perspectives are enigmatic because he was made at such a young age, but he has, like the other elders who have survived, learned to adapt to the changing cultural landscapes of Europe.

A crucial figure to Rice's revisionist history is Marius, an ancient Roman centurion who witnessed the great conquests of the empire, the conquering of the barbarians of western Europe, and the defeat of Rome at the hands of the barbarians of eastern Europe. More importantly, before he became a vampire, Marius was a historian. Marius was born to vampirism in the years of Augustus Caesar: "when Rome had just become an empire, when faith in the gods was, for all lofty purposes, dead." [11] So Marius's philosophy is to live a life without need for illusions or systems of rationalization; he has instead "a love of and respect for what is right before your eyes." [12]

Because of his status as an elder and the way Lestat presents him, the reader accepts the narrative reliability of Marius. However, even here, Rice subverts the reader's expectations. Marius, just like every other historian, has limited perspective and is subjective in his accuracy. Readers are first told the story of Akasha and Enkil (the original vampires) by Marius in *The Vampire Lestat*. [13] Only in the next novel, *The Queen of the Damned*, does the reader realize that he has left many gaps in the story. The history is revised when Khayman and then Maharet (both primary actors at the birth of the first vampires) narrate; we find out other things that were left out of Marius's version, because Marius heard the story so many hundreds of years after the fact. As Rice's narratives unfold, we are constantly invited to question historical narratives and note how they change with cultures and with narrators.

Rice even questions her own narrative and narrators. Louis narrates the first book of the series, *Interview with the Vampire;* in the second book, *The Vampire Lestat,* Lestat (as narrator) questions the reliability of the first book and advises the reader to "read between the lines." [14] This questioning, instead of creating cynicism or undecidability in the reader, serves to bind the books of the series together and lends more sympathy to Lestat as narrator. Unlike Louis, Lestat refers to himself as "I" and the reader as "you"—creating a symbiosis between them. He presents himself from many different angles: sometimes charming, fond, and delightfully nervy; at other times, he alters the lens just a little and crosses over into gloating, pettiness, defensiveness, score settling (which includes self-hate), and whining about his victimization. The trick is that somehow Lestat's personal style does cross the symbiotic bridge—elucidating widespread human traits and making his readers feel a little less lonely and freakish. [15] Lestat's texts, tied as they are to historical events, are further set up as real or reliable when Lestat makes comments about fiction:

> All during the nineteenth century, vampires were "discovered" by the literary writers of Europe. Lord Ruthven, the creation of Dr. Polidori, gave way to Sir Francis Varney in the penny dreadfuls, and later came Sheridan Le Fanu's magnificent and sensuous Countess Carmilla Karnstein, and finally the big ape of the vampires, the hirsute Slav Count Dracula, who though he can turn himself into a bat or dematerialize at will, nevertheless crawls down the wall of his castle in the manner of a lizard apparently for fun—all of these creations and many like them feeding the insatiable appetite for "gothic and fantastic tales." [16]

Another nexus of intertextuality between fiction and history appears as Rice folds mythical tales into the fabric of her vampire history; although myths are not history, they are historically, culturally, and oftentimes religiously bound. Rice connects many ancient myths to vampires. Perhaps the most important example is how the "Ones Who Must Be Kept"—the first father and mother (Akasha and Enkil)—take the names of the mythical Osiris and Isis because they believe ritual is a necessity for humans.[17] As they set themselves up as gods, the whole idea of religion and the origin of gods is questioned. Other myths are grafted into the narrative deal such as Dionysus, Attis, Cybele, Demeter, and Persephone.[18] In a story related by Marius, the religion of the Druids is also explained in terms of vampires being the worshipped ones. In fact, Marius's experience with the Druids is described as though it was an enactment of the ancient Greek harvest ritual.[19]

As Rice weaves together historical and mythical narratives with her own history of the vampires, the boundaries between these genres are blurred. One could say that she attempts too much and ultimately fails to deliver a "good" novel (this was most said by critics of *Queen of the Damned*). One could also say that as Rice blurs the boundaries of these genres that she questions, the placement of the boundaries becomes another postmodern methodology. Especially as the relationship between myth and religion becomes interrogated, Rice replaces foundational religious belief with mythical explanation. Rice's texts pose religion as a result of the need for ritual, and her character, Lestat, continues and transforms the ancient rites into a present-day context when he performs as a rock star: "Now I knew all that had been left out of the pages I had read about the rock singers—this mad marriage of the primitive and the scientific, this religious frenzy. We were in the ancient grove alright. We were all with the gods."[20] Marius explains the connected boundary more directly:

> As the Roman Empire came to its close, all the old gods of the pagan world were seen as demons by the Christians who rose. It was useless to tell them as the centuries passed that their Christ was but another God of the Wood, dying and rising, as Dionysus or Osiris had done before him, and that the virgin Mary was in fact the Good Mother again enshrined. Theirs was a new age of belief and conviction, and in it we became devils, detached from what they believed, as old knowledge was forgotten or misunderstood.[21]

Here Marius provides not only a revisionist historical account of religion, but an analysis of language. He goes on to describe a point in time when the word "evil" was attributed a new value: "when the Children of Darkness came to believe they served the Christian devil . . . they tried to give value to evil, to believe in its power in the scheme of things, to give it a just place in the world." Marius then offers an astute philosophical interpretation of history: "Hearken to me when I say: There has never been a just place for evil in the Western world. There has never been an easy accommodation of death. . . . The value placed upon human life has only increased. . . . It is the belief in the value of human life that carries man now out of the monarchy into the republics of America and France."[22] In passages such as these, Rice becomes much more than a writer producing entertaining Gothic tales; she addresses highly philosophical concepts while simultaneously blurring, questioning, and testing the boundaries between fact and fiction.

Issues of identity and history are not normally associated with the Gothic tradition. Usually ideas concerning a person's relationship with nature and God, the eternal nature of the human spirit and not the human body, and the values associated with Western morals and Christianity were (and still are) given a high priority. One has only to think of works such as Stephen King's *The Stand* and *Needful Things.* What Rice does differently is that she appropriates various conventions of the Gothic—the use of atmosphere, exotic locales, and supernatural beings—and places them in non-Christian postmodern settings. The Gothic concern about the transcendental (found for example, in *Frankenstein*—"There are some things that man should not tamper with") is transformed by Rice into a concern that humans always have preconceived notions of the universe, and that these notions lead us to believe differently about what should be tampered with and what should not. Unlike the more traditional work of King, in Rice's novels there is no god or devil (in the Christian sense). Therefore, there is no person or location where the reader can assign guilt or evil. Without valuative judgments, characters like Lestat or Lasher—so easily identified as evil in Gothic literature—become both good and evil. Even when they do traditionally "evil" things, the reader is still apt to identify and sympathize with the realistic complexity that makes up the personality of Rice's characters.

The Creation of Identity

> "You are the imitation of a man."
> —Marius

Rice's novel, *The Vampire Lestat,* is narrated by her most famous creation, Lestat de Lioncourt, who explains that his prose is bit of a "cross between a flatboatman and detective Sam Spade" with a French accent.[23] Lestat's struggles to accept himself as either evil or good, human or nonhuman, lover or monster, shape who he is. He has no identity of his own and does not know ethically what he is; he wishes he could believe that evil is a binary necessity because then he could just be happy about playing the monster—his best performance.[24] Since he has no place in any culture (even the one he is from), Lestat must construct his "self". He has no transcendental identity and no spiritual afterlife awaits him—his only soul is the one he makes. In the case of Lestat, his identity is constructed in performance by his desire to communicate through his roles as writer, rock star, vampire, and lover. He fashions not only himself, but also his philosophy—reasons and purposes for continuing to live—just as the old ones constructed mythologies around their powers and rituals to give them a place while adding human meaning to their existence. When Lestat first arrives in New Orleans, he writes about his marginalized position and his desire to belong somewhere:

> There were moments on that first night in this fetid little paradise when I prayed that in spite of all my secret power, I was somehow kin to every mortal man. Maybe I was not the exotic outcast that I imagined, but merely the dim magnification of every human soul. Old truths and ancient magic, revolution and invention, all conspire to distract us from the passion that in one way or another defeats us all. And weary finally of this complexity, we dream of that long-ago time when we sat upon our mother's knee and each kiss was the perfect consummation of desire. What can we do but reach for the embrace that must now contain both heaven and hell: our doom again and again and again.[25]

In the face of this dislocation, Lestat struggles between creating boundaries that allow him to "pass" as human and disregarding those boundaries in order to experience power and triumph over the passage of time.[26]

As "an immortal being who must find his own reasons to exist,"[27] Lestat's eternal quest is to find an identity he can "live" with. The identity forged for him by Rice, although Gothic in feeling, is postmodern in form. Lestat's first identity as hunter, or "wolfkiller," is given to him by his mother, Gabrielle. After being forbidden by his family to enter the monastery where he thinks he will belong, Lestat is forlorn until his mother brings him the clothes and weapons of a hunter; from this moment on, Lestat performs the role of wolfkiller. Later, he is excited by the emotions created by the traveling actors' troupe and wishes to fashion a new identity as Lelio, young lover to Isabella, in Paris's *Commedia dell'arte*. The acting career he chooses (although his family forbids him to continue) makes up his identity throughout the rest of the chronicles. Lestat performs—that is who he is. He soon finds out that fooling mortals into thinking he is human is just as easy as performing Lelio.[28]

Lestat is drawn to the actors because they create: "Actors and actresses make magic, they make things happen on stage; they invent; they create."[29] Musicians, like Nicki, receive the same esteem in Lestat's economy. Although he takes pleasure in his creativity as an actor with many roles, his cultural encoding makes it impossible for him to be at peace with these vampiric creations, which he still sees as immoral. He, therefore, constructs a philosophy (eclectically drawn from the writers of the cultures he has experienced) that allows him to justify his "art": "I took up the theme again that music and acting were good because they drove back chaos. Chaos was the meaninglessness of day to day life, and if we were to die now, our lives would be nothing but meaninglessness. . . . We are going to die and not even know. We'll never know, and all this meaninglessness will just go on and on and on. . . . How do you live, how do you go on breathing and moving and doing things when you know there is no explanation?"[30]

Lestat fills the void left by his question with art and materialism—the "art for art's sake" philosophy of the decadents. Therefore, any value ascribed to nature comes by way of its artistic value. When Lestat drinks innocent blood for the first time, he describes his vision as a garden of savage beauty: "[It] had been a true vision. There was meaning in the world, yes, and laws, and inevitability, but they had only to do with the aesthetic."[31] The philosophies and justifications that Lestat develops, however, continue at odds with the ethical encoding of his primary culture. As he continues to question his purpose and meaning, his identity resists cultural boundaries and is reforged and changed. Only at the end of his last book does Lestat seem to grasp the idea that his is not a transcendental self, but a constructed self.

As he closes *The Tale of the Body Thief*, Lestat writes: "Yes, say something—for the love of heaven and the love of Claudia—to darken it and show it for what it is! Dear God, to lance it and show the horror at the core. But I could not. What more is there to say, really? The tale is told."[32] Lestat's inability to go deeper—to find what is at the core—

exists not because he is unable to dive deeply enough, but because there is no core. The telling of the tale, the performance of it, is his only meaning. Lestat struggles with this question of the interiority and exteriority of identity. Finally, at the end of his latest book, he seems to come to an understanding that his performances (whether vampire, monster, lover, son, rock star, master, friend, wolfkiller, or actor) are his self-definition. What he has been doing as he dons his many roles is the ritual of creating meaning and testing boundaries.

Another boundary that Lestat is compelled to push against is the limitations, or the lack of limitations, of his body. Rice's concentration on the body, the sensuous, and the sexual becomes progressively more important with each novel. In the early chronicles, Lestat often describes the physical in sexual terms. Like Bram Stoker's *Dracula,* Rice's characters become sexually irresistible when they are reborn as vampires; the moral judgment against this sexuality is, however, missing in Rice. Her discovery and celebration of the sexual body is reminiscent of the early days of liberal American feminism, in which women discovered that controlling their bodies means having control of their selves. Rice, however, goes a step further and, like postmodern feminists, connects the importance of the body to identity formation—to gaining agency through "subject-hood."

Lestat learns of the connection between himself as subject and his body in the last book of the chronicles, *The Tale of the Body Thief.*[33] The phrase "body and soul" recurs throughout this novel—from David Talbot's idea that God is absolutely body as well as soul to Raglan James's explanation of the way to switch bodies: one's soul rises up from its body, leaves behind a "residual soul," and then takes possession of another body. This is the concept upon which the book is based as Lestat leaves his own vampiric body to take possession of a human one. He learns that the boundaries of the human flesh that he has been romanticizing about for so long are more problematic than he remembers, and he realizes that his vampiric body and its physical abilities and limitations are undeniably an inseparable part of who he is. In this last narrative, Lestat perhaps learns the lesson Pandora had shared in an earlier tale ("If the mind can find no meaning, then the senses give it. Live for this, wretched being that you are") and that even young Claudia had tried to teach ("Let the flesh instruct the mind").

Unlike her readers, Rice's characters have been forming an identity since the first days of recorded time. In this way, Rice's self-fashioned characters are caught up in redefining the manners of many cultures.

Perhaps Rice will get her wish for immortality; her textual creatures have entered the *zeitgeist* of the twentieth century, and will live on—not only as vampires, mummies, spirits, and witches, but also as cultural philosophers, storytellers, critics, and historians.

Notes

1. This is now especially true with the 1994 release of *Interview with the Vampire,* directed by Neil Jordan and starring Tom Cruise and Brad Pitt (TriStar).

2. Rice replies to these critics playfully in *The Tale of the Body Thief,* in which Lestat writes: "I already know of course that I am sensuous, florid, lush, humid—enough critics have told me that" (4).

3. The Gothic novel is usually defined as a tale of the macabre, fantastic, and supernatural set amidst haunted castles, graveyards, ruins, and wild picturesque landscapes. The word "Gothic" originally meant "medieval," as in Walpole's *The Castle of Otranto: A Gothic Story* (generally accepted as the first Gothic novel). Its use of ghosts and graveyards, living statues, and mysterious appearances helped to further define the genre. Later works such as Beckford's *Vathek* with its emphasis on demonic possession and torture became so extravagant that they became the subject of parody for writers such as Jane Austen *(Northanger Abbey)* and Peacock *(Nightmare Abbey).*

4. Anne Rice, *The Mummy, or Ramses the Damned* (New York: Ballantine, 1989) 157.

5. Rice, *Mummy* 153.

6. Rice, *Mummy* 154.

7. Rice, *Mummy* 116.

8. Rice, *Mummy* 202–3.

9. Anne Rice, *The Vampire Lestat* (New York: Knopf, 1985) 61.

10. Rice, *Lestat* 276.

11. Rice, *Lestat* 333.

12. Rice, *Lestat* 333.

13. Rice, *Lestat* 380–87.

14. Rice, *Lestat* 435.

15. Phillip Lopate, *The Art of the Personal Essay: An Anthology from the Classical Era to the Present* (New York: Doubleday, 1994) xxxii.

16. Rice, *Lestat* 436.

17. Rice, *Lestat* 388.

18. Rice, *Lestat* 356.

19. Rice, *Lestat* 351.

20. Rice, *Lestat* 470.

21. Rice, *Lestat* 404.

22. Rice, *Lestat* 404–5.
23. Rice, *Lestat* 4.
24. Rice, *Lestat* 15–16.
25. Rice, *Lestat* 430.
26. Rice, *Lestat* 407.
27. Rice, *Lestat* 331.
28. Rice, *Lestat* 100.
29. Rice, *Lestat* 45.
30. Rice, *Lestat* 49, 51.
31. Rice, *Lestat* 124.
32. Rice, *Lestat* 430.
33. In Rice's most recent series, *The Witching Hour*, *Lasher*, and *Taltos*, the importance of the body in the construction of identity is perhaps even more prominent. The "spirit" Lasher who has stayed with the Mayfield family of witches through several centuries wishes for, more than anything else, a body. This, however, should be the subject of a much longer essay.

5

Mirror and Labyrinth
The Fiction of Peter Straub

Bernadette Lynn Bosky

Peter Straub's fiction is notable for its combination of unity and variety: the continuing exploration of specialized themes and a characteristic tone within works that cover a range of settings, genres, and styles. While this is not necessarily unusual—in fact, it characterizes most good artists in any field—it may be less common than it should be among writers of the modern American Gothic, especially due to economic pressures to stay in one genre-marketing niche. Straub is not prolific, but each piece of work, especially from *Ghost Story* to the present, is a significant new step in the development of his oeuvre; Straub is not so much looking for his voice as he is choosing to explore different vehicles for different aspects of it and working each approach both thoroughly and inventively.

Broadly, Straub's career as a writer falls into four sequential divisions. His first published work was poetry, including material in the leading literary magazine *Poetry* in 1970 and 1971, and a collection entitled *Open Air*, published by Irish University Press in 1972. In 1983, Underwood-Miller issued a selection of Straub's poetry, *Leeson Park and Belsize Square*. Straub wrote two mainstream literary novels: *Marriages*, published in 1973, and *Wild Animals*, begun in the early 1970s, but not published until 1984. (The latter novel lent its name to an omnibus of Straub's novels, but was reissued by itself as *Under Venus*.) These novels show the influence of his experience with poetry, but also contain some elements found later in his novels.[1]

Straub first became widely known as a novelist of supernatural horror. His agent, Carol Smith, proposed that he "write a gothic," partly in order to "make some money for a change." "I said, 'What's a gothic?'—

and I still don't know," Straub states. Yet he realized that he had been both enjoying and telling horror stories most of his life.[2] The first result of this suggestion was *Julia,* published in 1975 (dates given throughout this chapter are for paperback publication). Straub continued this direction with *If You Could See Me Now* (1977); hit his stride with *Ghost Story* (1979) and *Shadowland* (1980), and concluded this approach with *Floating Dragon* (1982); *The General's Wife,* a piece originally intended for that novel but published on its own (1982); and *The Talisman* (1984), co-written with Straub's friend and mutual influence, Stephen King.

After that, Straub felt he needed "to take some time off," and that he had already done "everything [he] needed to do with the materials of horror."[3] The result was the Blue Rose series: *Koko* (1988), *Mystery* (1990), and *The Throat* (1993), and the novellas "The Blue Rose" (1985) and "The Juniper Tree" (1988). Taken together, these "form, in effect, one massive story" written in and about the genres of mystery and detective fiction.[4] His works from *Julia* through *The Talisman* were based in the Gothic tradition and the modern supernatural horror genre. In a pattern of shifting references characteristic of Straub's writing, the phrase "Blue Rose" refers not only to a set of unsolved murders, but also to a piece of jazz music, a nonsense utterance to induce an hypnotic trance, and the wallpaper an abused child would concentrate on while being molested.

In 1990, Straub's only collection of shorter fiction, *Houses Without Doors,* was published. This contains, and is dominated by, the Blue Rose novellas. The collection shows a synthesis of all of Straub's approaches to fiction from the realistic New York setting and characters in "The Buffalo Hunter" to the indeterminacy—certainly surreal and probably supernatural—of pieces including that novella, the novella "Mrs. God" (also available in a longer form published separately by Donald Grant) and the early work, "Something About a Death, Something About a Fire."

The style and tone of Straub's fiction, while consistently recognizable, also shows much variation; to some extent, the style of each book is based on the models within its chosen genre. Thus, *Marriages* and *Under Venus* are literary and even poetic in diction and emphasis, as well as in subject matter; Straub describes *Marriages* as "sort of like that Renata Adler book, *Speedboat,* except that it was a little more coherent."[5]

Within the Gothic genre of supernatural horror, Straub plays with a number of styles from such specific influences as Henry James, whose lessons about the nature of horror dominate *Julia* and help shape *Ghost*

Story; Nathaniel Hawthorne, who influences *Ghost Story* and is referred to in *If You Could See Me Now;* British short-story writer Robert Aickman, along with Carlos Fuentes' *Aura* an influence on "The General's Wife" and later basic to "Mrs. God"; and Stephen King, whose influence is most evident in the structuring of *Ghost Story* and in the clear style and operatically loud events of *Floating Dragon.*[6]

Elsewhere, the style of Straub's work is more shaped by examination of a kind of writing than it is influenced by a specific author, as in his use of the Anglo-American nineteenth-century supernatural tradition in *Ghost Story;* detective and mystery fiction in the Blue Rose books; and European fairy tales in *Shadowland* (which features the Brothers Grimm as minor characters) and in the Blue Rose works such as "The Juniper Tree" and *The Throat.* A contrast of *Shadowland* and *The Throat* shows how Straub can use similar source materials to achieve different thematic and literary effects.

In some ways, this variety of genre templates can obscure the ways in which Straub has mixed genres throughout his career. All of his fiction uses realistic and literary approaches. Moreover, all of his fiction from *Julia* on includes horror and Gothic conventions to some extent, and all of it includes realistic mysteries concerning murder, paternity, and theft. Both the proportion of these elements and the genre-expectations Straub plays upon, however, do change.

Straub's works also show quite a range of approaches to plot and structure—though this seems to be less a matter of turning to different, but equally useful, alternatives and more a matter of Straub's abilities developing throughout his career. *Julia* is neat and controlled, but mainly because its scope is restricted. The novel is a straightforward narrative (with the past revealed as events progress) of a drawing-room sized ensemble. From *If You Could See Me Now* through *Shadowland,* Straub widened the plans for his novels, but the effects on plot and structure were mixed—sometimes well orchestrated, as in the arrangement of exposition and plot threads in *Ghost Story,* and sometimes loose or arbitrary, as in the climaxes of *If You Could See Me Now* and *Shadowland* or the long interpolated narrative by Coleman Collins in the latter book. Straub's approach in these novels is often associational and imagistic, perhaps influenced by his interest in jazz music.[7]

Though it is often accused of being sloppy, because it is the most violent and colloquial of Straub's books, *Floating Dragon* is actually more carefully structured than its predecessors. In this respect, it may be a turning point for Straub. From *Julia* on, Straub has shown an interest in undermining a strictly linear sense of time in order to explore a Gothic sense of the eternal consequences of some actions. In *Floating Dragon*, this is conveyed through the novel's organization. Central episodes (often moments of revelation or recognition) are referred to both before and after they are presented; these references radiate throughout the text and create an impression of connections among otherwise unrelated actions.[8] On the other hand, *The Talisman* needs a more elaborate and careful interweaving of events in order to connect and counterpoint our world and the Territories. This may be a result of King and Straub's streamlining the book, after the outline had been written, to make it a publishable length.[9]

Certainly by the time he wrote the Blue Rose books, Straub had learned how to make plot and structure fundamental assets of his fiction—as one might expect of someone writing mystery and suspense fiction. Not only does Straub develop plot and maintain interest by the careful apportioning of facts and events, he also demonstrates an ongoing process of sifting truth and falsehood by revisiting and revising material from earlier in the books. *The Throat*, especially, is an impressive performance with many convincing false endings and well-planned surprises. As Tim Underhill says in that novel, "These books are about the way the known story is not the right or the real story."[10] Thus, in the Blue Rose books as in *Floating Dragon*, Straub uses plot and structure to convey theme as well as to move the story.

Certain approaches do characterize all of Straub's fiction, despite differences in genre, style, and plot. One obvious, but very interesting, approach is his use of factual elements in his often-fantastic fiction—especially places and situations from his own life.[11] This strategy is, of course, very common. Still, it is valuable to look at how the author manages the interplay of autobiographical influence and fictional inventions. Straub does so in three main ways: the use of factual background to give credibility to entirely or primarily fictional characters and situations; the concrete depiction of the author's personal hopes and fears, or issues to be worked out; and the use of various versions of places and events to provide a kind of referential layering that draws attention to the relationship between fact and fiction in a postmodern, metafictive way.

A quick review of Straub's life shows how much he has mined his experiences to provide convincing, yet often unusual, settings and events for his books. He spent summers with relatives in the Norwegian rural area near Arcadia, Wisconsin, which provides the setting—altered to the worse—of *If You Could See Me Now*. The prep school he attended in Milwaukee appears, again in more sinister form, as Carson School in *Shadowland*. In each case, the novel explores emotional and social issues related to the setting: the burden of small-town familiarity in *If You Could See Me Now*, the challenge of individuation in *Shadowland*,[12] and the menace of smug and petty authority in both books.

After receiving a bachelor's degree in English from the University of Wisconsin and a master's degree in contemporary literature from Columbia University, Straub taught English for three years; this background shows in a number of places in Straub's works, especially in the Don Wanderly and Alma Mobley scenes in *Ghost Story*. In 1969, he began work on a Ph.D. at University College in Dublin; while working on an unsatisfactory dissertation on D. H. Lawrence, like Miles Teagarden in *If You Could See Me Now*, Straub began writing professionally. His experiences in academics can also be found in works such as *Mrs. God*. Straub's feelings about the academic life seem ambivalent—perhaps one reason why those settings lend themselves well to his brand of Gothic fiction.

Straub moved from Dublin to England before writing *Julia*, which reflects the new location. Similarly, *Floating Dragon* was written while Straub lived in Connecticut and takes place in a similar Connecticut town. Straub's understanding of place allows him to show the darkness behind even the most respectable town. As a character in *Floating Dragon* says, "I say this isn't *sub*urbia, and it isn't *ex*urbia. It's *dist*urbia."[13] In "The Buffalo Hunter" and the Blue Rose books, Straub shows his knowledge of and affection for the locations and cultures of New York's Manhattan.

Straub's use of this source material, however, reaches a new level of complexity and sophistication in the Blue Rose books. *Mystery* takes place on the Caribbean island of Mill Walk, and *The Throat* takes place in the town of Millhaven, Illinois; both may ultimately be based on Milwaukee, Wisconsin, where Straub was born in 1943, and which appears as a minor setting in *Koko*. Similarly, Tom Pasmore's near-death experience in *Mystery* is revealed by Tim Underhill in *The Throat* to be his; and in real life, Straub also was badly injured in a childhood accident: "a really transforming experience."[14] The Blue Rose books also include more topical references and events than Straub's earlier books—from the Vietnam War Memorial in *Koko* to Milwaukee serial killer and cannibal Jeffrey Dahmer, clearly behind Walter Dragonette in *The Throat*.[15]

Yet if we are tempted to take Straub's fiction as autobiographical, or as a breakable code, we are warned against doing so by the other obvious source of material equally evident in all his work: other fiction. Even in *The Throat*, Straub mentions Tom Flanagan (the protagonist of *Shadowland*, or the real-life jazz musician, or perhaps both)—and, more to the point, Arkham College, a nod to H. P. Lovecraft's fictional Massachusetts town. Like the character in "The Buffalo Hunter," Straub's readers may ultimately give up on sorting out fact and fiction—though presumably without the fatal emergence of fiction into real life that is portrayed in that novella. Still, fiction in the universe of Straub's works is always both desirable and dangerous. Fiction always lies, Straub seems to say, especially in the Blue Rose books; and it always tells the truth.

Beginning with *Ghost Story*, Straub combines straightforward action and suspense with a strong awareness of and metafictive play with his literary roots. Preparing to write *Ghost Story*, Straub took six months to read and reread the classics, including works by Edgar Allan Poe, Ambrose Bierce, Edith Wharton's ghost stories, J. Sheridan Le Fanu, nineteenth-century novelist Mrs. Gaskell, Arthur Machen, H. P. Lovecraft and his circle, and a number of continental supernatural books.[16] The most important references in *Ghost Story* are to James and Hawthorne, whose last names are shared by the two main characters in the novel; Straub even includes a retelling of *The Turn of the Screw* by one of the characters.

Even more interesting are the nonsupernatural works which influenced Straub's supernatural novels: John Fowles's *The Magus* is the text-behind-the-text in *Shadowland*;[17] and Mark Twain's works are central to *The Talisman*,[18] as prefigured by Straub's use of "I Light Out for the Territories" as the title of the second half of *If You Could See Me Now*. The latter novel combines references to a surprising range of authors from D. H. Lawrence to H. Rider Haggard.

Straub, who describes himself as "probably the only guy who sees Henry James and [Raymond] Chandler on an equal plane," turned to the genre of the latter in the Blue Rose books; he has mentioned the influence of Daphne Du Maurier on *Mystery*, and Ross McDonald on *The Throat*.[19] In addition, *The Throat* mentions the television show *Twin Peaks* and Thomas Harris's novel *Red Dragon*.[20] These contemporary references place the characters believably in our world, but also offer homage to those works that explore themes seen in the Blue Rose books such as exposing the town's corruption in *Twin Peaks*, the psychology of the serial killer explored in Harris's novel, and the complex questions of identity and duplicity/doubles in both.

In *Mystery*, Straub examines the two main schools of mystery writing—the more action-oriented American school and the more intellectual detective work of Sherlock Holmes and his kin. The latter is represented by Lamont von Heilitz, a self-described "amateur of crime"[21] who approaches crimes as puzzles to solve; the former is carried by a number of lesser characters including police chief Tim Truehart and detective David Natchez. Apprentice detective Tom Pasmore, who comes of age in *Mystery*, realizes "that there were two ways of being a detective, and that men like David Natchez would always find people like von Heilitz too whimsical, intuitive, and theatrical to be taken seriously."[22] In *The Throat*, Tom Pasmore has taken over von Heilitz's role; he contrasts himself to the "brilliant street detective" Paul Fontaine, whose abilities seem better fitted to our current semi-random serial killings.[23]

Other references and motifs in the Blue Rose books are drawn from the Grimm's fairy tale, "The Juniper Tree," and from classical mythology (particularly the figure of the minotaur hidden in a labyrinth). Straub also refers to the Pandora myth in many of his works—including *If You Could See Me Now*, *Ghost Story*, and *Shadowland*.[24] Especially in *Koko*, "The Juniper Tree," and *The Throat*, these form two basic metaphors for repression or estrangement and recovery or reintegration: literally, dismembering and remembering along with burial and discovery.[25]

As in *Shadowland*, which also refers to fairy tales and some classical myths, the use of these materials in the Blue Rose books fits with their exploration of basic questions of identity and change. Straub has mentioned that Bruno Bettelheim's study, *The Uses of Enchantment*, led him to see that "fairy tales were often parables of the construction of the personality,"[26] so it is fitting that Tom Flanagan, Tom Pasmore, and Tim Underhill would see themselves through these stories, and that Straub would use the stories and myths as patterns for their development. He achieves a similar effect in *The Talisman* through the use of heroic or quest literature; "like the story of Jesus, the story of King Arthur, Sir Gawain and the Green Knight."[27]

Perhaps Straub's least successful metafictional pattern is seen in the use of Biblical material in *Floating Dragon*. The illness and madness that beset the town are explicitly compared to Old Testament punishments;[28] and the age-old menace, Gideon Winter, is repeatedly referred to as an apocalyptic, or satanic, "old dragon." There is more to this Biblical imagery than first meets the eye, and it does give the book a compelling feeling of ancient sin; but it never seems as well done, or as thematically important to the work, as Straub's use of literary materials in his other fiction. Perhaps the true text-behind-the-text in *Floating Dragon* is Stephen King's fiction. However, if this is true, Straub does not make it explicit or use it as a source of metafictive play, as he does with influences in the other books.

These metafictive concerns in Straub's books combine well with another characteristic of all his fiction: the frequent use of imagery, which functions as a unifying leitmotif and advances tone and theme. The best example of this is probably the bird imagery throughout *Shadowland;* one could also point to the spreading irradicable stain the heroine encounters in *Julia,* the bat and dragon imagery in *Floating Dragon,* and even the fixation on baby bottles by the protagonist in "The Buffalo Hunter." As the final example shows, such imagery permeates not only the authorial language of the works, but also the events as facts within the story. In the Blue Rose works, dismemberment, underground journeys, and eating form metaphors in which the characters both think and are described; they are also echoed in actions and locations that occur in the novel.

One motif stands out as omnipresent in Straub's works: the woods, which serves as a place of wild possibility and danger. In *If You Could See Me Now,* Miles Teagarden feels a panic in the woods, "an essentially literary experience, brewed up out of Jack London and Hawthorne and Cooper and Disney cartoons and Shakespeare and the brothers Grimm."[29] This depiction recurs in various forms such as imagery and location in *Ghost Story, Shadowland, Floating Dragon,* and *The Talisman;* even *Under Venus* concerns the selling of forest land. The major templates are the Puritan experience of the seemingly endless forest at their backs in *Floating Dragon* and the story of Hansel and Gretel in *Shadowland.*[30] In the Blue Rose books, the underworld has in many ways replaced the forest, but some of the events in *Mystery* convey these same feelings about the woods and "The Juniper Tree" explicitly refers to Hansel and Gretel.

Straub's main characters tend to be urbane and somewhat self-aware, but often very ordinary in temperament, even when they are thrust into extraordinary circumstances or possess extraordinary abilities. The protagonists in his earlier supernatural novels tend to be weaker and more neurotic, but still a kind of everyman or everywoman; beginning with *Ghost Story,* the protagonists start out better balanced and mature or grow stronger through the events of the book. Straub has always been drawn to characters who are themselves artists and thinkers, including the musician-protagonist of *Under Venus*, von Heilitz and Tom Pasmore in the Blue Rose books, semi-effectual semi-scholars Miles Teagarden in *If You Could See Me Now* and Martin Standish in "Mrs. God," and the whole range of writers: Don Wanderley in *Ghost Story*, Graham Williams in *Floating Dragon*, the narrator of "The Juniper Tree," and Straub's "co-author" and major figure in the Blue Rose books, Tim Underhill.

In some ways, these characters show Straub writing about what he knows—we cannot assume they are self-portraits, but they certainly reflect the life that Straub has led, rich in thought rather than adventure. His characters may also be shaped by Straub's strengths as a writer since his style and detailed examination of inner life require a thoughtful, and even self-absorbed, protagonist. Finally, the contemporary novel of supernatural horror—unlike some of its exotic Gothic ancestors—usually requires the credibility that comes from common characters the reader can identify with.

Straub's characters frequently are involved in a search for an absent father or the escape from an evil father. In both *Shadowland* and *The Talisman*, the young man who will mature into adulthood during the novel has lost his father to death just before the story begins. In *Shadowland*, what is offered as a replacement is the magician Coleman Collins—a controlling manipulator Tom rejects. In *The Talisman*, bad father-figures abound—from Jack's uncle, Morgan Sloat, to the despot-like owners of the Oatley tavern and the Sunlight Home for Boys. These characters are often overdrawn and lack the credibility Coleman Collins sometimes has. Moreover, a criticism of contemporary realistic fiction seems implied when the villains are named Smokey Updike and Sunlight Gardener, but little or nothing is accomplished with this, compared to the rich tapestry of references in *Shadowland* or *Ghost Story*.

Both Tom in *Shadowland* and Jack in *The Talisman* benefit from the assistance of protectors and advisors (someone between friend and father). Both benevolent men are African-American, and each has a dual nature: Bud Copeland/Speckle John for Tom, and Speedy Parker/Parkus for Jack. In both books, those who offer to be replacement fathers are evil, while true mentors think of themselves more as helpers.

The matter of "fathers and sons"[32] is central to *Floating Dragon*, especially seen in Richard Albee's absent father (ironically reflected by the situation-comedy Richard acted in as a child, *Daddy's Here*) and Tad's abusive father. Finally, the strains and joys of the father-son relationship are shown by the benevolent trigenerational relationship of

Tad, Richard, and Graham Williams at the end of the novel. That configuration is reminiscent of the relationships among Peter Barnes, Don Wanderly, and the remaining members of the Chowder Society in *Ghost Story*. Don comes to the town of Milburn, New York, to investigate his uncle's death. As he takes his uncle's place in the storytelling group of old men called the Chowder Society, the other members become his true family.

In the Blue Rose books, Straub explores issues concerning abusive fathers (and abusive father-like authority figures); weak or absent fathers like Mr. Pasmore in *Mystery;* and the question of true paternal heritage, which any wise child seeks to know—a question which also forms the central mystery of *Julia*. Perhaps the most touching real father in Straub's fiction is April Ransom's in *The Throat*. Beset by senility (which Straub depicts all too convincingly), he rallies himself to mourn his dead daughter and even helps provide information that identifies her murderer.

From *Julia* through *Floating Dragon*, Straub's novels tend to be structured around a constellation of four major characters—often united by guilt over a past incident, by the need to fight a supernatural menace, or both.[33] *Shadowland* presents the tetrad of Del, Tom, Rose, and Cole; but that novel and *The Talisman* are more noteworthy for the doubling or pairings. In each book, the basic unit is the dyad—Tom and Del, Jack and Wolf replaced by Jack and Richard—and primary and secondary characters have a dual nature that is both mundane and mythic: Rose Armstrong, girl and mermaid; the butler Bud Copeland, who may or may not be Speckle John; and all the "twinners" in *The Talisman*, who exist both in this world and in the Territories.

Paired characters are also important in the Blue Rose stories, especially in the relationship between von Heilitz and Tom Pasmore in *Mystery* and the teamwork of Pasmore with Tim Underhill in *The Throat*. In "The Juniper Tree," the protagonist and the man in the theater form a poisonous, but deeply bonded, dyad. Each is also split into two or more selves as they hide the secret of sexual abuse not only from the outside world, but also, by repression and dissociation, from their own minds.

Beginning with *Ghost Story*, Straub explores questions of identity by presenting both different characters who somehow seem connected to one another or share some fundamental characteristic, and single characters who seem to split into many apparitions or selves (comparable to what Todorov calls "the multiplication of personality").[34] Often Straub establishes such connections through the depiction of one figure who appears under many different names or different characters with the same initials: the sinister blonde child in *Julia;* the many alluring and frightening females with the initials A. M. in *Ghost Story;* and perhaps even Graham Williams, dragonslayer, and Gideon Winter, his adversary, in *Floating Dragon.*

In *If You Could See Me Now*, Miles Teagarden returns to his hometown for a rendezvous with his dead sweetheart, Alison Greening, and meets his cousin's daughter, Alison Updahl, who resembles her physically as well as in name; toward the end of the novel, Miles signs his own name as "Miles Greening." The Blue Rose stories bloom with a multifoliate multiplicity of similar, linked, opposed, and transforming characters as intricate as the more supernaturally complex identities in *Ghost Story, Shadowland,* and *Floating Dragon:* murder suspects William Damrosch and Walter Dragonette in *The Throat;* the permutations on F. B. and L. V. in that same book; and the vast range of criminals, detectives, and writers who populate the three novels and two novellas.

Just as Straub's strength as a writer shows in his handling of shifting, overlapping, and connected identities among his characters, all of his books demonstrate an impressive ability to depict a wide variety of states of consciousness. Even the early mimetic novels explore unusual emotional and mental states. In *Julia* and *If You Could See Me Now*, Straub uses the freedom that the supernatural provides to experiment even further; by *Ghost Story*, this has become a permanent and vital part of his approach.[35] The supernatural novels examine personal consciousness and our awareness of reality as altered by movies, fiction-reading, trances, hallucinations, dreams, magic, and pathological symptoms such as depersonalization and mood disorders. The Blue Rose stories also use some of these approaches, and also add abuse-related dissociation, war as an initiation and an altered state (hinted at in *Shadowland*, but not fully explored), the near-death experience, and use of recreational drugs.

The blending of objective and subjective states in Straub's novels enhances the fiction in a number of ways. The characters' inability to tell what is real and what is not is itself frightening, yet often fascinating; moreover, in dissolving usual boundaries between reality and illusion, Straub makes it easier for his readers to believe the supernatural events of the novel. In depicting extreme or borderline states, Straub can use techniques from the introspective, realistic literary novel while still providing a Gothic excitement. Finally, such scenes may cause the reader to reevaluate some questions of epistemology and even phenomenology;

this deeper speculation especially fits *Ghost Story*'s concern with the nature of the self, and the gnostic or Hermetic themes in *Shadowland*.

Straub's interests in identity and consciousness may be revealed in his use of mirrors, which both reveal and alter the self, especially to the perceiving self. This thematic significance seems implicit in the mirrors of *Floating Dragon* and "The Juniper Tree", and is made explicit in the narcissist imagery in *Ghost Story*. Stephen King, in his perceptive impressionistic critique of *Ghost Story*, writes that this is not only the nature of mirrors, but also the nature of ghosts: "What is the ghost, after all, that it should frighten us so, but our own face? When we observe it we become like Narcissus." Straub's ghosts—like those in *The Turn of the Screw*—are based in this awareness, which is a large source of their power.[36] In the Blue Rose books, the characters face interior ghosts which are often no easier to exorcise, just as haunting, and also found in the mirror. Ransom states in *The Throat*, "the world is full of ghosts, and some of them are still people."[37]

In all his fiction from *Julia* on, Straub uses these techniques and others to examine two basic ideas about, or thematic approaches to, the world around us. One is that time is not truly linear and that isolation of an event in the past or future is no barrier, for good or ill, from its effects. The other is the gnostic or Hermetic idea that the world we know could be a false show and the true world lies waiting to be discovered.

Both of these are often presented in spatial metaphors. In *If You Could See Me Now*, Miles states, "Effects can leak backward and forward in time, staining otherwise innocent events."[38] As we have seen, this is enacted in the structure of *Floating Dragon*—although the events can have good reverberations as well as bad—and is represented in that novel by Tabby, who has visions of the past, and Patsy, who is only precognitive. Finally, "backwards and forwards" is a refrain of the eponymous character in *Koko* that reflects his helpless view of time.[39] Another spatial metaphor for this effect appears in *Koko* in the events in the cave at Ia Thuc: "the center was the center, which was the secret, and the power of what Harry Beevers had felt and done radiated out through the rest of his life."[40] This metaphor also permeates both the events and the structure of that novel.

Straub also describes the hidden reality as being behind or beneath the reality we know. Miles explains in *If You Could See Me Now* that the world we know is "the rind," peeled off to reveal dark truths within[41]— true reality "broke through the apparently real like a fist."[42] Coleman Collins realizes that the magic of Shadowland "had been there all along, right under the surface of things, dogging me";[43] and Koko thinks, "There is no jungle but the jungle, and it grows beneath the sidewalks, behind the windows, on the other sides of doors."[44] In *The Throat*, awareness comes from dangerous depths behind and—like the minotaur that represents everything the protagonist represses—beneath the world we know.[45]

Finally, Straub's fiction is often seen in terms of connections or patterns—a spatial metaphor that completely abandons sequence. This image is most prevalent in *Julia* and *Floating Dragon*, but is also used in *Ghost Story*. In *If You Could See Me Now*, Miles thinks, "I saw the patterns tying us together," and notes another character's mention of "lines of force."[46]

Often in Straub's books, the secret world revealed to the characters is horrible—like A. M. in *Ghost Story* when she reveals her true, inhuman form. In *Mystery*, Tom Pasmore learns from his nurse that "the world is half night";[47] and in *The Throat*, Tim Underhill thinks, "The world is half in night, and the other half is night, too."[48] Yet, as Tom Flanagan, Tom Pasmore, and Tim Underhill all discover, the secret world can also be a source of wonder and glory. As gnostic quotation reads in both *Shadowland* and *The Throat*, "If you bring forth what is within you, what you bring forth will save you; if you do not bring forth what is within you, what you do not bring forth will destroy you."[49] This secret, hidden in ourselves and in the world, can heal as well as horrify.[50]

In Straub's fiction, this secret is often connected to the nature of women and to sex as a gateway to mysteries that are transcendent and exciting, but also frightening and sometimes dangerous. The strongest connection between *Under Venus* and Straub's other work is this aspect of the protagonist's mistress, Anita Kellerman. Most of Straub's female characters share some of this nature—powerful, inscrutable, alluring, and intimidating:[51] Alison Greening of *If You Could See Me Now*, *Shadowland*'s Rose Armstrong, Patsy at the climax of *Floating Dragon*, and even Maggie Lah in *Koko* and *The Throat*. The most outstanding example is the female shapeshifter in *Ghost Story*—purely destructive, yet alluring with "a morally fatal glamour";[52] but Don Wanderley, also says, "all women are mysteries to me."[53]

Straub's books from *Julia* on also explore the power of the past, whether personal, as in *Julia*, or historical, as in *Floating Dragon*. Often, the personal and social are combined, as in *If You Could See Me Now*, *Ghost Story*, and the Blue Rose stories. Many works by Straub link personal decline or salvation, sometimes based on guilt from the past, to the decay or redemption of a town *(Ghost Story, Floating Dragon)*, a small community (the school in *Shadowland*), or even a world *(The Talisman)*. In *If You Could See Me Now* and the Blue Rose books, personal salvation lies—in part—in uncovering the town's innate corruption and in apportioning guilt and innocence correctly.[54]

As Straub writes in *If You Could See Me Now* and *Koko*, "No story exists without its past, and the past of a story is what enables us to understand it."[55] This powerful past is sometimes embodied, in a very Gothic way, in a house or place that haunts the novel and its characters: the house Julia feels compelled to buy, the one Miles Teagarden moves into and refurnishes as it had been when Alison Greening was alive, the houses of Eva Galli in *Ghost Story* or Bates Krell in *Floating Dragon*, the schools in *Shadowland* or *The Talisman*, the theaters from *Ghost Story* and *The Throat*, the cave at Ia Thuc, or the room under the Green Woman Taproom.

After the many developments in Straub's career, even a critic—who is presumptuous by profession—should know better than to anticipate his next move. Some clues may lie in interviews: despite the mixed success of movies based on *Julia* and *Ghost Story*, films may be made of *Floating Dragon* (a script by William Nolan exists) and *The Talisman* (although Steven Spielberg is no longer likely to direct). Straub is currently writing, and he may do a project "loosely based on *Rogue Male*, the Geoffrey Household novel."[56] However, his planned novels have mutated while in progress before,[57] and any solid predictions would be foolhardy.

General observations seem both safer and more valuable. In some ways, *The Throat* combines realistic detective fiction with more supernatural elements, which might show an approaching synthesis in Straub's future work. We can probably expect consistent themes and approaches—including uses of metafictive and autobiographical material—explored in books with new developments in tone, structure, and perhaps even genre. Or perhaps not. In any event, it will be enjoyable to read, and well worth analyzing and appreciating.

Notes

1. Bernadette Bosky, "Peter Straub: From *Academe* to *Shadowland*," *Discovering Modern Horror Fiction II*, ed. Darrell Schweitzer (Mercer Island: Starmont House, 1988) 3–4; Paul Gagne, "An Interview with Peter Straub," *American Fantasy* (Feb. 1982): 10.

2. Jay Gregory, "TZ Interview: Peter Straub," *Twilight Zone Magazine* May 1981: 13–14; Gagne 10.

3. "Peter Straub: The Path of Extremity," *Locus: The Newspaper of the Science Fiction Field* Jan. 1994: 4.

4. *Locus* 4.

5. Gagne 10.

6. Bosky, "Peter Straub" 4, 12–15; Bernadette Bosky, "Stephen King and Peter Straub: Fear and Friendship," *Discovering Stephen King,* ed. Darrell Schweitzer (Mercer Island: Starmont House, 1985) 58–62; Gregory 14; Gagne 15; Stephen King, *Danse Macabre* (New York: Berkeley, 1981) 250; Peter Straub, *The General's Wife* (West Kingston: Donald M. Grant Inc., 1982) 21; Peter Straub, *Houses Without Doors* (New York: Dutton, 1990) 357.

7. Bosky, "Stephen King" 62–63; Gregory 15–16; Gagne 23.

8. Bosky, "Stephen King" 62–63.

9. Douglas Winter, "Stephen King, Peter Straub, and the Quest for *The Talisman*," *Twilight Zone Magazine* Jan.–Feb. 1985: 139–42; Bosky, "Stephen King" 68.

10. Peter Straub, *The Throat* (New York: Dutton, 1993) 46.

11. Bosky, "Peter Straub" 3–4; Gagne 8–26; Gregory 13–16.

12. See Edwin F. Casebeer, "Peter Straub's *Shadowland:* The Initiation of a Magician," *The Journal of the Fantastic in the Arts* forthcoming.

13. Peter Straub, *Floating Dragon* (New York: G. E. Putnam Sons, 1982) 173.

14. Michael Berry, "Horror Talks with Peter Straub," *Horror: The News Magazine of the Horror and Dark Fantasy Field* Jan. 1994: 93; see Bernadette Bosky, "Theseus in Millhaven," rev. of *The Throat* by Peter Straub, *Necrofile: The Review of Horror Fiction* 9 (1993): 4–5.

15. *Locus* 65.

16. Bosky, "Peter Straub" 8; King, *Danse* 244; Jennifer Dunning, "Behind the Best Sellers: Peter Straub," *New York Times Book Review* 20 May 1979: 56; Gagne 14–15.

17. Gagne 18; Bosky, "Peter Straub" 12.

18. Tony Magistrale, "Science, Politics, and the Epic Imagination: *The Talisman*," *The Dark Descent: Essays Defining Stephen King's Horrorscape* (Westport: Greenwood Press, 1992) 115–19.

19. Berry 91–92.

20. Straub, *Throat* 255.

21. Peter Straub, *Mystery* (New York: Dutton, 1990) 81.

22. Straub, *Mystery* 515.

23. Straub, *Throat* 255.

24. Peter Straub, *If You Could See Me Now* (New York: Pocket Books, 1976) 157; Straub, *Ghost Story* (New York: Pocket Books, 1980) 137, 144; Peter Straub, *Shadowland* (New York: Berkeley, 1981) 176–78.

25. Bosky, "Theseus" 5.

26. Gagne 18.

27. Winter, "Stephen King" 66–67; William Goldstein, "A Coupla Authors Sittin' Around Talkin'," *The Stephen King Companion*, ed. George Beahm (Kansas City: Andrews and McMeel, 1989) 286.

28. Straub, *Floating Dragon* 290.

29. Straub, *If You Could See* 137.

30. Straub, *Floating Dragon* 114, 389; Straub, *Shadowland* 18.

31. Peter Straub, *The Juniper Tree* 87.

32. Straub, *Floating Dragon* 538.

33. Bosky, "Peter Straub" 9.

34. Tzvetan Todorov, *The Fantastic: A Structural Approach to a Literary Genre*, trans. Richard Howard (Ithaca: Cornell University Press, 1975) trans. of *Introduction à Littérature Fantastique* (Paris: Seuil, 1970) 107–20.

35. Bosky, "Peter Straub" 4, 10–12, 14.

36. King, *Danse* 246–48.

37. Straub, *Throat* 75.

38. Straub, *If You Could See* 107.

39. Straub, *Koko* (New York: Dutton, 1988) 343, 345, 553.

40. Straub, *Koko* 500.

41. Straub, *If You Could See* 321.

42. Straub, *If You Could See* 99.

43. Straub, *Shadowland* 291.

44. Straub, *Koko* 502.

45. Straub, *Throat* 136, 219, 431–41.

46. Straub, *If You Could See* 309.

47. Straub, *Mystery* 43.

48. Straub, *Throat* 655.

49. Straub, *Shadowland* 327; Straub, *Throat* 140.

50. Bernadette Bosky, "Haunting and Healing: Memory and Guilt in the Fiction of Peter Straub," *The New York Review of Science Fiction* Sept. 1994.

51. Bosky, "Peter Straub" 7, 8, 10, 11.

52. Straub, *Ghost Story* 378.

53. Straub, *Ghost Story* 301.

54. Bosky, "Haunting" 11–13.

55. Straub, *If You Could See* 17; Straub, *Koko* 81.

56. Berry 93–94; *Locus* 65.

57. Berry 91.

6

Casting Out Demons
The Horror Fiction of William Peter Blatty

Douglas E. Winter

"If there were evil spirits, why not good?
Why not a soul? Why not life everlasting?"

A single novel, published in 1971, changed the course of contemporary American horror fiction and film. Praised, maligned, and misunderstood, William Peter Blatty's *The Exorcist* was not simply a commercial juggernaut, spending some fifty-five weeks on the *New York Times* bestseller lists, but also a cultural phenomenon that confronted mainstream America with ideas and imagery that previously had been discounted as the stuff of fringe "occult" fiction and "B" movies. More than any entertainment before—and, arguably, since—*The Exorcist* unleashed the genie of transgression from the bottle of the repressed American psyche. Along with its gentler kin, *Rosemary's Baby* by Ira Levin (1967) and Thomas Tyron's *The Other* (1971), this novel ushered in the reign of Stephen King and the stylized genre of horror that swept this country in the late 1970s and early 1980s. Its immensely popular motion picture adaptation—in whose shadow the novel has languished—redefined the visual experience of horror by elevating special effects to roles as crucial as those of actors.

Ironically, Blatty, who authored both the novel and the film adaptation of *The Exorcist*, had not previously written what he prefers to call "ghostly" fiction. Although well-established as a novelist and screenwriter, with eight published books and eleven produced film scripts before *The Exorcist*, Blatty was known as, of all things, a writer of comedy.

His first foray into professional writing came at about age ten, when he won five dollars in a twenty-five-words-or-less contest for *Captain Future* comic books. He wrote: "Gentlemen: I like Captain Future Comics because it's about the world of tomorrow, and anything about the world of tomorrow is interesting." [1]

Only the world of tomorrow could be interesting to young Bill Blatty, for the world of his childhood was a difficult one. Born 7 January 1928, on the verge of the Great Depression, he was the fifth child of immigrant Lebanese parents; his father, a carpenter, left home when Blatty was six years old. It was a time of "flexible living"—his mother peddled homemade quince jelly on the streets of New York City, and in the space of ten years the family lived at twenty-eight different addresses. At school, he was an outsider often set upon for his peculiar name and dusky complexion.

His religious upbringing was rigorous and Roman Catholic. "My mother was a deeply religious woman, very devout. I attended Catholic grammar school, St. Stephen's, in New York; Brooklyn Preparatory, a Jesuit High School; and Georgetown University, also a Jesuit school. As Loyola, or one of the early Jesuits, is reputed to have said, 'Give me the boy, and the man will be mine forever.' I think that's true. There's no such thing as a former Catholic." As for his personal belief system: "I'm a relaxed Catholic. I think Catholicism is as close to the truth as any organized religion has come, and I look forward to the day when the more daring of the theoretical physicists nudge Catholicism into some sort of amalgamation with the philosophic insights of the Eastern religions."

Blatty escaped the harsh realities of his childhood through the fantasies of comic books, pulp magazines, and radio plays like *The Shadow* and *Captain Midnight*. It was the pulps that inspired him to become a writer. When he read "Time Wounds All Heels," an early Robert Bloch story in *Unknown*, "I just fell apart with laughter, and I would call my friends and read the entire story to them. And I caught fire. I wanted to write something like that. And I started trying comedy, because it was the laughs that got me."

After graduation from Georgetown University in 1951, he joined the U.S. Air Force and was assigned to his parents' homeland, where his looks and fluency in Arabic gave him entrée to humorous episodes reflecting the clash of American and Middle Eastern cultures. While later obtaining a master's degree in English literature from Georgetown and pursuing a career in public relations, he wrote a series of articles for the

Saturday Evening Post and *Coronet* based upon his experiences—one of which involved him posing as the son of King Saud—that served as the groundwork for his first novel, *Which Way to Mecca, Jack?* (1960).

"It all happened in a very Horatio Algerish way. . . . An editor at McGraw-Hill wrote to me and said, 'I've been following your work. Have you ever thought about writing a book?' And I said, 'Oh, yes, I've been thinking about that'—for, my God, since puberty!" He began writing *Which Way to Mecca, Jack?* and, while ghostwriting a celebrity advice-to-the-lovelorn book, offered the manuscript to his publisher. "One little irony is that the book that I ghosted was a raging bestseller; of course, the one written under my own name was not."

Blatty talked his way onto Jack Paar's "Tonight Show" to promote *Which Way to Mecca, Jack?* and his humor brought him the attention of a film producer. "Columbia had decided to shelve a treatment for a projected comedy film, and he wanted me to take another crack at it, looking toward writing a script. I did, and they decided to make the movie—*The Man from the Diner's Club* with Danny Kaye. Since then, I've just stayed one or two steps ahead of the sheriff."

Blatty quickly became one of Hollywood's leading comedy writers, scripting *Promise Her Anything* (1962); *John Goldfarb, Please Come Home!* (1963), based on his novel of the same name; *What Did You Do in the War, Daddy?* (1965); and *The Great Bank Robbery* (1967). He worked extensively with Blake Edwards, writing one of the earliest and best "Pink Panther" movies—*A Shot in the Dark* (1964)—as well as *Gunn* (1967) and *Darling Lili* (1968). During this intensely prolific decade, Blatty also wrote the novels *I, Billy Shakespeare* (1965), and *Twinkle, Twinkle "Killer" Kane* (1967). His reputation for comedy was so distinct that the cover of *"Killer" Kane*—his first "serious" novel, intended to explore the mystery of goodness—featured a *New York Times* quotation: "Nobody can write funnier lines than Bill Blatty."

Then, in 1967, his mother died suddenly, and Blatty became disillusioned with Hollywood and its increasingly bureaucratic view of the screenwriter. In early July 1969, he rented a cabin in the woods near Lake Tahoe, intending to take a break and write a new book. His life—and the modern horror novel and film—would be changed forever.

The Exorcist had its beginnings twenty years earlier, during Blatty's junior year at Georgetown University. He had read, in the 20 August 1949 edition of the *Washington Post,* a news report about a Catholic priest's exorcism of a fourteen-year-old Mount Rainier, Maryland, boy allegedly possessed by the devil. The account confirmed what Blatty had heard from one of his Jesuit instructors, Father Eugene Gallagher. His reaction was not one of fear, but of wonder:

> First of all, I believed every word that Father Gallagher reported. And I thought, "Oh, my God. At last, proof of transcendence, or at least the reality of spiritual forces." I mean, intelligent, discarnate entities—demons, devils, whatever. It seemed a validation of what we were being taught as Catholics, and certainly a validation of our hopes for immortality. Because if there were evil spirits, why not good? Why not a soul? Why not life everlasting?
>
> Well, that excited me. And I thought that it would be wonderful if someone were to investigate the case and write a nonfiction account. But I never connected myself as the one who should write it. I was going to be an English teacher in those days.

(A nonfiction study of the incident, Thomas B. Allen's *Possessed: The True Story of an Exorcism,* was not published until 1993.)

As the years passed, Blatty's interest in the possibility of demonic possession continued, and he collected information on the subject as a pastime. Early in the 1960s, he proposed to write about the case, but neither his agent nor his publisher favored the idea. At a New Year's Eve dinner in 1967, a conversation with Marc Jaffe, the editorial director of Bantam Books, convinced Blatty that he should write a book. Despite his religious background, he was skeptical of the published accounts:

> They were far removed in time, for the most part; or, if not removed in time—like the case in Earling, Iowa, in 1928—the account seemed to have been written by an overly credulous and pious nun, although it was written by a religious brother. I was just extremely skeptical. I was like Thomas—I needed to put my own fingers in the wounds. So I started digging, trying to find the exorcist in the 1949 case; and Father Gallagher gave me the name— Father William Bowdern.
>
> I wrote to him, but he wrote back and said that he had promised the family of the victim that there would never be any publicity and that there would be complete secrecy. This piqued my interest, because the usual nut case is dying for publicity. And he said, "The only thing I can tell you is that the case I was involved in was the real thing. I had no doubt about it then, and I have no doubt about it now."

I felt the blood prickling up my back as I read those words. And, of course, I wrote him a very impassioned letter as to why the greatest thing for the Catholics would be to have a book of this kind written. I proposed that perhaps he should write it—again, I was still thinking it should be nonfiction. He reiterated that he would simply have nothing to do with it. And then he begged me to write nothing that would connect the victim to the case, because it would be deeply traumatic to the boy and to his family. That's why, when I wrote the book, I changed the boy to a girl. I changed the location.

The essential plot of *The Exorcist* is now etched into the public consciousness, but the novel deserves to be read, and read again, since time has not tarnished its reputation as an instant classic of American horror fiction. Although occasionally overwrought and susceptible to sprawling asides—particularly when compared with the lean prose of Blatty's earlier and later novels—*The Exorcist* succeeds through a nervous style that mingles mystery with metaphysics, hard science with sensationalism. In retrospect, the novel is noteworthy for what it is not: certainly it is not the flat out horror film later scripted by Blatty and directed by William Friedkin; and, indeed, its literary precedents are those of detective fiction rather than those of horror.

In an enigmatic prelude, a nameless man in khaki, working the archaeological digs at Nineveh in northern Iraq, foresees the coming of an ancient evil. Cut to Georgetown, the ever-trendy section of Washington, D.C., where divorced actress Chris MacNeil and her eleven-year-old daughter Regan have taken up temporary residence during location shooting for a new film. It is 1 April—April Fool's Day—and Chris hears strange noises in the attic: "What looked like morning was the beginning of endless night."[2]

Chris (whom Blatty based on his friend, actress Shirley MacLaine) is an atheist haunted by the death of her only other child. Regan is a model daughter—"Red ponytails. Soft, shining face full of freckles"[3]—but she is lonely. Hurt by her parents' divorce, she retreats into a dreamworld of Ouija boards and imaginary friends. The minor annoyances of the house shift into dramatic changes in Regan: insomnia, rebelliousness, rapping sounds, furniture moving, and other increasingly strange gestures for attention. When Burke Demmings, the alcoholic director of Chris's film, falls to his death down Georgetown's famous "Hitchcock steps," Chris fears that Regan is somehow responsible. As Regan's mental condition deteriorates into inexplicable rampages and obscenity, a battery of physicians eliminate pathological causes and recommend a psychiatric solution; and finally, in one of horror fiction's more subversive sequences, it is the doctors who at last tell Chris MacNeil to seek supernatural intervention—an exorcist.

Enter Father Damien Karras—Jesuit priest, a psychiatrist, and a counselor to fellow priests—who has been placed on leave because of his own difficulty in coping with the death of his mother. Spiritually exhausted, wracked with doubt and guilt, Karras takes the Host in Mass, only to find "the papery taste of despair."[4] He yearns for some sign of the existence of God: "In the world there was evil. And much of the evil resulted from doubt; from an honest confusion among men of good will. Would a reasonable God refuse to end it? Nor reveal Himself? Not speak?"[5] When Karras confronts Regan's trauma, he can find no evidence of anything but mental disorder.

The central tension of the novel, then, is whether Regan McNeil is possessed by demons—and if so, why. This tension is multiplied through the sublime irony of pairing an atheist mother who believes desperately that her daughter cannot be insane—and thus can only be possessed—with a Jesuit priest who denies the possibility of the supernatural and searches for rational explanations that grow ever more far-fetched: split personality, telepathy, psychokinesis. Blatty then inserts a third factor into the equation: the Jewish homicide detective William Kinderman, a rumpled investigator whose unremittant *schmaltz*—"pawing at truth like a weary bachelor pinching vegetables at market"[6]—cloaks a street-smart, intuitive, and persistent investigator whose eyes are open to any explanation.

When at last Father Karras, like the other psychiatrists, believes that an exorcism may work some psychological magic on Regan, he presents his evidence to the church. The novel then turns full circle: the man in khaki from the prelude is revealed as Father Lankester Merrin, an aged priest who once conducted an exorcism in Africa and who is now summoned again to do battle with the ageless evil that has entered into the innocent Regan. Modeled on the Jesuit philosopher-paleontologist Pierre Teilhard de Chardin, Merrin is everything that Karras is not—a true believer who is singleminded in his purpose—but he also hides his own secret: a failing heart.

It is Merrin who explains to Karras, and thus the reader, why such a violent and obscene horror has descended upon this innocent child: "[T]he demon's target is not the possessed; it is us . . . the observers

. . . every person in this house. And I think—I think the point is to make us despair; to reject our own humanity, Damien: to see ourselves as ultimately bestial; as ultimately vile and putrescent; without dignity; ugly; unworthy. And there lies the heart of it, perhaps: in unworthiness. For I think belief in God is not a matter of reason at all; I think it finally is a matter of love, of accepting the possibility that God could love *us*. . . ." [7]

Although forgotten in the wake of the motion picture—which proceeded from the given that Regan McNeil was possessed—the readers of 1971 were confronted with a novel that posed a medical and spiritual dilemma, and that left repeated loopholes for rational explanations offering an abundance of red herrings. Not until its final fifty pages did the novel confirm its supernatural reality.

Although less than elegant in its early chapters, *The Exorcist* weaves a tangled web of mystery and metaphysics, and it is one of a handful of contemporary supernatural novels to confront religious issues in a thought-provoking manner. A more sly and subtle subtext, unnoticed by the reviews of the time, was the novel's play on crucial social issues: women's liberation and the rebellion of youth. Here was a dramatic suggestion that a woman's devotion to her career rather than the home might leave her child vulnerable—spawning the ultimate delinquent: a demon. Chris McNeil is reminded repeatedly that what has happened to Regan must somehow have resulted from a lack of attention or reliance on the care of others; and when Chris shouts "that thing upstairs is not my daughter" [8] she echoes the sentiments of an entire generation of parents whose children grew their hair long, listened to loud rock-and-roll, and dabbled with drugs and revolution.

Nevertheless, it was the sensationalism of *The Exorcist*—its full-throttle assault on a gauntlet of taboos and its resurrection of the obscene from the realm of pornography—that enthralled readers in the millions. The inevitable motion-picture adaptation, with an Academy Award-winning script by Blatty, stunned the nation. The spectacle of a young girl's possession, rendered in the first unleashing of graphic makeup effects (presided over by Dick Smith) in a big-budget film, set the media abuzz with debates about exorcism, horror, and morality. Moviegoers ran shrieking from theaters, and there were even claims that viewers had been possessed by demons. The Reverend Billy Graham pronounced: "There is a power in the film that is beyond the film."

To this day, Blatty is bemused by the reaction to *The Exorcist*, and disappointed that its horrific elements overpowered his spiritual message. "With the film, the people were just getting the rollercoaster ride. Let's face it—the message was adroitly snipped out of the film. On the most basic level, the film argues for some kind of transcendence: If there are demons, why not angels? Why not God? And one religion, the Catholic Church—if not others as well—seems to have power to command the evil spirit, which seems a validation of religious belief. But the real point of the book is nowhere to be found in the film." Friedkin's ambiguous climax (in which Father Karras, after summoning the demon into him, leaps from the window to his death) caused many filmgoers to believe that the demon had triumphed; but his decision to excise Father Merrin's explanation of the possession is more lamentable. It was this scene that justified the extremes of the film and that rendered the sensational into the spiritual.

In both book and film, *The Exorcist* brought not only a huge audience, but also a new legitimacy to horror; in publishing and filmmaking parlance, horror was profitable and worthy of pursuit. It did not make writers like Stephen King and Peter Straub possible, for they were well on their own way to success; but it certainly attuned American readers to a new horror—one that was contemporary, brash, bold and, above all, entertaining; and one that felt free to enter the neighborhoods, the homes, the very bedrooms of suburbia in pursuit of the darkening American dream.

Yet Blatty declined to take what, for some, seemed the inevitable next step: a sequel or, at the very least, another horror novel. Instead, he delivered *I'll Tell Them I Remember You* (1973), a nonfiction memorial to his mother. "My publisher took it because I wanted to do it, and they were looking ahead to my next novel. But the bookstores were really hostile. . . . Then Warner Brothers offered me a lot of money if I would agree to write the sequel to *The Exorcist*. I didn't. But frankly speaking, I wish I'd done it now. Then at least we would never have had *The Heretic*."

Blatty is quick to divorce himself from John Boorman's disastrous motion picture: *Exorcist II: The Heretic* (1977). Blatty refused to write the screenplay and lobbied the studio against making the film. When asked to authorize a novelization of the film, he refused despite a sizable financial offer. "The only suggestion I made was after I saw *The Heretic* . . . I called the producer and suggested that they retitle it *Son of Exorcist*, that they give me the film and allow me to write some additional funny dialogue and dub it in and well, you know, go with it. He hung up the phone on me."

Blatty finally wrote his sequel, *Legion* (1983), but more than ten years after *The Exorcist*—years marked by two marriages and two children, but very little writing. Indeed, his only published work was a revision of his short novel *Twinkle, Twinkle "Killer" Kane* as *The Ninth Configuration* (1978). He then scripted and directed a motion-picture version that won the Golden Globe Award for best screenplay of 1981.

The Ninth Configuration is a brief, erratic tragicomedy that merges the sensibilities of Joseph Heller's *Catch-22* (1961) and Ken Kesey's *One Flew Over the Cuckoo's Nest* (1962) in an exploration of the innate goodness of people. The novel is set in a Gothic mansion in the American northwest that serves as a hospice for officers who, without any history of mental illness, manifest sudden psychoses when facing combat in Vietnam. A renowned but idiosyncratic Marine psychiatrist, Colonel Hudson Kane, takes command of the facility and confronts its funfair of patients, whose ringleader is the wisecracking astronaut Cutshaw and the only inmate to falter during a peaceful mission—a moon launch.

Amidst comic vignettes, including the efforts of a B-52 navigator to train dogs to perform Shakespeare, Kane and Cutshaw argue physics and metaphysics—each searching in his own way to make sense of evil. The title of the novel refers to the dissymmetrical configuration of a protein molecule whose existence would be necessary for life to appear spontaneously on earth; Kane finds its mathematical probabilities more fantastic than a belief in God. He ruminates: "I think about sickness; earthquakes, wars. . . . Painful death. The death of children. Children with cancer. If these are just part of our natural environment, why do they horrify us so? Why do we think of them as evil unless . . . we were programmed . . . for someplace . . . else? . . . Maybe conscience is our memory of how things were. Just suppose that we *haven't* evolved; that we've really been going backwards . . . more and more alienated from"—here Kane stops, because "Psychiatrists aren't supposed to say 'God.' "[9]

Kane pushes himself to exhaustion and despair at the seemingly impossible task of aiding his wards: "I don't think evil grows out of madness: I think madness grows out of evil."[10] Eventually he encourages their flamboyant acts because he believes that his patients have avoided insanity by feigning insanity—that the crazier their behavior, then the nearer they will come to health and to God. "Maybe everything evil is a frustration, a separation from what we were meant for. . . . And maybe guilt is just the pain of that separation, that—that loneliness for God. We're fish out of water . . . maybe that's why men go mad."[11]

In a sudden twist, it is revealed that the doctor is actually "Killer" Kane—a legendary guerilla warfare specialist who lost his nerve after the decapitation of a Vietnamese child. Assigned to the hospital by mistake—it is his brother who is a Marine psychiatrist—Kane has obeyed the orders and seeks to do penance for his killing by curing.

When Cutshaw enacts a fantasy of escape and breaches the gates of the mansion, Kane pursues him to a rundown tavern, where a biker gang has assaulted the helpless astronaut. "Here's your goodness in man," the bloody Cutshaw tells Kane,[12] but Kane takes his place and allows the bikers to beat and humiliate him until at last he can take no more: "Killer" Kane rises from his darkness and murders four of the gang members before taking his own life—a sacrificial lamb. The shock of Kane's death restores many of the inmates to sanity. Kane leaves a letter for Cutshaw that offers an explanation of why God does not simply appear and end the confusion about his existence: "It is not what we see in the sky that helps; it is what is in the heart: a right hope, a good will."[13]

Despite its Gothic trappings, *The Ninth Configuration* is an uneasy fusion of comedy and polemic: wry one-liners, argumentative asides, surreal tomfoolery, and a suddenly serious finale confound the reader. Blatty's fundamental concern—the problem of good—is diffused by the comic interludes, and both the content and style of his conclusion seem torn from the pages of a different book. The novel is clearly a transitional work, a stopgap that signaled a more powerful bookend to *The Exorcist*—a sequel that seemed, by the close of the 1970s, not merely inevitable, but inescapable: "Though [*The Exorcist*] poses the problem of evil and glancingly suggests a few rather tired old answers, [it] does not give an answer that is satisfying or intellectually convincing. It wasn't until the point at which I determined to write *Legion* that I finally had the answer—a really satisfactory answer to the problem of evil."

Legion is not, at first glance, a traditional sequel. The MacNeils are ancient history—distant faces in the endless parade of homicide investigations that have confronted Lieutenant William Kinderman in the twelve years since the exorcism and the death of Father Damien Karras. On the anniversary of that fateful day, Kinderman ponders a crucified child who is the latest victim to bloody the streets of Washington, D.C. The corpse bears the signature atrocities, some known only to the police, of a serial killer known as Gemini; but the Gemini Killer has been dead for more than a decade.

In *The Exorcist*, the garrulous and eccentric Jewish detective was a minor player who disposed of false leads and offered occasional comic relief; but in *Legion*, Kinderman takes center stage. Blatty again works in the style of a mystery. Indeed, this novel is a classic police procedural, although the grumpy tenacity of his detective's investigation is interspersed with increasingly obsessive ruminations on the problem of evil. Kinderman's thoughts are timely ones, for evil—an ancient evil—is loose again. In time, a chain of murders links two impossibilities: the Gemini Killer and the exorcism that took place twelve years earlier.

When Father Dyer, another background character in *The Exorcist*, is killed in Georgetown Hospital, Kinderman finds his way into the deepest lair of the psychiatric ward where an amnesiac, found wandering the streets more than a decade before, has been kept; his catatonic state has only recently been relieved. The patient, known only as Mister Sunlight and locked down securely, announces that he is the Gemini Killer. Although Sunlight—whose conversations with Kinderman anticipate those of the infamous Hannibal Lecter in the novels of Thomas Harris—knows the intimate details of the murders, he wears the face of Father Damien Karras. An exhumation of Karras's grave reveals the body of an elderly priest. Kinderman is drawn inescapably to a solution that is both horrifying and yet somehow transcendent. At the moment of death, it would seem, Karras was possessed by the forces of darkness; for Mister Sunlight is indeed Karras in body. But in mind? Kinderman, like Jesus Christ, asks the man his name; and he receives the time-honored answer: "Legion, for we are many." [14]

Again, Blatty withholds the supernatural explanation until his final pages by offering up a compelling alternative theory that is purely rational and steeped in psychiatry. Unlike *The Ninth Configuration*, this novel successfully integrates metaphysical argument with a compelling fiction—principally because the character of Kinderman is so well realized that his penchant for pondering the existence of a God who would allow evil and suffering is not simply forgivable but comfortable—and, in time, actually propels the story forward.

At heart, *Legion* is an unabashed polemic that presents an intriguing theory of the supernatural that does explain the problem of evil: if this world is interpenetrated by another, then the "Fall of Man" is really the fall of some immensely powerful and luminescent being—in Biblical terms, the angel Lucifer—in whom humanity is somehow incorporated. We are part of the body of that being and are finding our way back toward God.

This theory is only slightly removed from the orthodox religious concept of original sin in the Garden of Eden.

> I find it satisfying. . . . I would think that someday very orthodox religious thinkers and theologians might come to embrace it, because it makes a great sense out of some nonsense that orthodoxy has to try to explain, and they usually have to start explaining it to children in the second grade of Catholic school. . . . Do you mean to tell me, Sister Evangeline, that because one person did a bad thing, every child who is ever to be born on earth is going to be physically crippled and bear the so-called "stain" of Original Sin? Every child is going to be vulnerable to being born with cancer? Have to endure not only illness but earthquakes and the thousand other natural calamities that the human body is subject to in this savage world?
>
> But if Adam and Eve—metaphorically you and I, every one— are parts, individual parts, of one luminous personality, to undergo what we now call "suffering," that's perfectly plausible. That's understandable. Now I know why I might get cancer, even though innocent.

Blatty wrote and directed an exceptional motion picture adaptation of *Legion* that, in order to satisfy its producers, wore the uncomfortable title *Exorcist III* (1990). Like the original film, *Exorcist III* downplays the essential religious argument of its source material; but it is a masterful exercise in restraint, as Blatty inverts the sensationalism of his predecessor. With a painstaking sense of atmosphere, he delivers sublime moments of *frisson* by alluding to, but never truly showing, extreme physical violence. It is clearly a writer's film driven by dialogue and evoking emotions deeper than those of shock; and it is marred only by a special-effects laden finale, again demanded by Hollywood moneymen.

Hidden, but not lost entirely in the motion picture adaptations of *The Exorcist* and *Legion,* is the uneasy juxtaposition of fear and hope that powers the novels. The films capably deliver the horror, but the metaphysical triumph that is central to Blatty's novels is subdued. Thus, *Exorcist III* lacks the intriguing subplot of *Legion* (which involves the experiments of a prime murder suspect, Dr. Amfortas, who listens patiently for the voices of the dead to appear on tape recordings of silence). Blatty, who has tried this high-tech version of the Ouija board, wonders aloud at how the sound of a voice on a tape recording made in an empty room could instill the emotion of fear: "Mine is one of tremendous elation. If there really is something manifesting on that tape—and God knows whether there is or not—then that is one more piece of evidence for the continuity of our lives, for survival after bodily death. What is frightening about that?"

For William Peter Blatty, the dialectic of horror is a supremely serious one; although he entertains, he refuses to offer escape. His horror fiction confronts the existence and meaning of the supernatural—and, in turn, the existence of that elemental aspect of our humanity that knows good and distinguishes it from evil. The rarity of his vision and the insistence with which he explores the light within the darkness place him among a handful of writers who seek, through the wounded Gothic that is the contemporary American horror novel, an answer to the riddle that is God. Although his trilogy of metaphysical mystery novels is sparse in words, it is a legacy that is long on thought and that ranks with crucial prominence among the horror fiction of our time.

Notes

1. All quotations from William Peter Blatty are taken from personal interviews with Douglas E. Winter.

2. William Peter Blatty, *The Exorcist* (New York: Harper & Row, 1971) 44.

3. Blatty, *Exorcist* 23.

4. Blatty, *Exorcist* 49.

5. Blatty, *Exorcist* 48–49.

6. Blatty, *Exorcist* 136.

7. Blatty, *Exorcist* 311.

8. Blatty, *Exorcist* 214.

9. William Peter Blatty, *The Ninth Configuration* (New York: Harper & Row, 1978) 25–26.

10. Blatty, *Ninth Configuration* 26.

11. Blatty, *Ninth Configuration* 26.

12. Blatty, *Ninth Configuration* 116–17.

13. Blatty, *Ninth Configuration* 12.

14. Mark 5:9.

7

Adam's Dream
The Gothic Imagination of Whitley Strieber

Mary Pharr

"The Imagination may be compared to Adam's dream—
he awoke and found it truth."
John Keats

To Whitley Strieber, humankind exists in a perpetual paradox: an isolation chamber with the door wide open. Within this confined space men and women live with a false sense of security created by their refusal to believe that anything exists outside the cell itself. When the chamber is invaded by strangers who simply come through the open door, most of its inhabitants refuse to acknowledge them as real. Essentially, Strieber sees humanity holding itself in solitary confinement by an unwillingness to consider even the possibility of other sentient beings. It is not daily reality that keeps people isolated; it is the determination to ignore whatever comes from beyond that reality.

Virtually all of Strieber's work hinges on the crucial renunciation of this isolation—a renunciation that leads first to a recognition of the strangers at our door and then to an awareness that their impact on our lives is likely to be both extensive and profound. The human ability to explore this impact is tested throughout Strieber's canon with varying results. For the task is a huge one requiring an imagination open to the truth of the mystery that G. R. Thompson has called "the perception of a world that stretches away beyond the range of human intelligence— often morally incomprehensible—and thereby productive of a nameless apprehension that may be called religious dread in the face of the wholly *other*."[1] In his own life, Strieber seems determined to experience this indefinable awe as a kind of romantic communion with the numinous, but in his fiction he presents it as more Gothic than romantic. The tension between these perspectives is what gives Strieber's work its force.

As a sensibility, romanticism has a huge advantage in a secular world: like a religion (but without dogmatic restrictions), it allows a man or woman to find a place in the universe by acknowledging a kinship with whatever else exists. The romantic perspective sees the universe as organic rather than mechanical. If everything in the cosmos is connected just as the smallest leaves of a tree are joined to its unseen roots, then everything—including everyone—has a kind of symbiotic value. Strieber claims to have found such value for himself—with the implication being that if he can find it, so can his audience. Yet, what his work reveals is as much Gothic shadow as romantic illumination. For the Gothic is the antithesis of romanticism that suggests not a symbiotic kinship with the others of the universe, but a predatory relationship that can never be in balance. If the romantic self joins harmoniously with the surrounding others to form a whole, the Gothic self trembles alone, in constant danger of losing all identity while being absorbed by a more powerful and fundamentally malign other.

So it is that in Strieber's fiction, the strangers who intrude on humanity's self-imposed seclusion not only dwarf the scope of daily life, but also offer enlightenment at the risk of destruction. By overcoming skepticism and opening themselves to that risk, Strieber's most successful characters (including his own narrative persona) are able to look up from their solitude and see the universe as it is—predatory, hard, and painful, but uncircumscribed by the narrow parameters of isolation and confinement. Hence the final twist of the paradox: to ignore the strangers at the door is to remain ignorant of the nature of the universe; to acknowledge them is to become aware of the nature of fear.

During an interview with Douglas E. Winter published in 1985, Strieber said, "Fear is the basis of existence"[2] and the dominant emotion in the inevitable movement toward death. But Strieber also sees fear as a natural way to make people alert—conscious of the fact that predation is essential to "the justice of the universe."[3] There is no point in giving in either to despair or condemnation when looking at a natural predator, because everything that exists uses something else that also exists to survive. Whatever morality there may be in such a tough universe is concerned with control. Reckless predation reflects a self-destroying, reality-denying hubris that is not only suicidal, but utterly abhorrent.

The willingness to look for such hard truths is at the core of Strieber's importance as a writer. There is something eminently modern about him: a man who seeks the universal but who questions the universalities he proposes. In his fiction, Strieber has personified his search by showing the tangled dealings between human beings and the archetypes of horror: werewolves, vampires, witches, assorted demons and monsters, and even a serial killer. But in *Communion* (1987), his capstone work, he goes beyond all other Gothic writers to challenge consciously the boundaries of fiction and fact. Shaman or charlatan, he shares those famous contrary qualities of Lord Byron: "too idealistic to refrain from blowing bubbles, and too realistic to refrain from pricking them."[4]

In his first published novel, *The Wolfen* (1978), Strieber presents his canon's themes with a maturity amazing for a first book (a maturity developed, perhaps, through the nine rejected novels that preceded it). Strieber traces the origin of *The Wolfen* to a midnight stroll in Central Park during which he realized he was being followed by a pack of wild dogs.[5] Out of this incident he developed the *Canis Lupus Sapiens*, not wolves but Wolfen—an intelligent, sensitive species of predator that has evolved alongside (but for the most part unknown) to humans. As always, *Homo Sapiens* refuses to believe that anything in any respect superior to humanity can live on this planet, and so humankind perceives the Wolfen as mere animals or ancient myths. For predators, this is an ideal situation: both in rural and urban areas, they can hide as needed and feed on the old and the lost without risk. By creating a society of transience and blight, human beings have made themselves the perfect prey.

But the prey is not stupid, only arrogant and ignorant. Nor are the Wolfen perfect: like all creatures, they err through misjudgment and excess. Two yearlings foolishly kill a couple of policemen who have inadvertently wandered into their lair. The ensuing investigation gradually reveals the truth. As one of the investigators notes, "All of history mankind has been living in a dream, and suddenly we're about to discover reality."[6] Understandably terrified, the police refer to the Wolfen as werewolves—legends now revealed as facts. With their superb sensory capabilities, adequate body language, advanced mental capacity, and familial devotion, the Wolfen are well equipped to survive in a nontechnological world. But the world that has discovered them is highly technical. Whether the two species can coexist in full knowledge of each other is debatable. If they cannot, it is a toss-up which will inherit the earth.

Strieber splits his narrative between the human and the Wolfen points of view, leaving reviewer Barbara Bannon to marvel at the way this author "conjure[s] up a certain amount of sympathy and compassion for the Wolfen, horrendous as they are."[7] What is, perhaps, as remarkable is that Strieber conjures up equal sympathy for the humans in his story, whose actions over history have been at least as horrendous as those of the Wolfen, and who are emphatically less compassionate toward one another and the earth. In the police protagonists, Wilson and Neff, Strieber shows a man and a woman who try to remain open to discovery even when what they find utterly unnerves them because it reverses their sense of who is master of the planet: "Man had always confronted nature by beating it down. This was going to require something new—the werewolf would have to be accepted."[8] In effect, the detectives realize something their narrow-minded, politically-oriented bosses do not: humankind is not the measure of all things. That revelation is repeated, with increasing urgency, throughout Strieber's canon.

In *Wolfen*, Michael Wadleigh's 1981 film version of the novel, Wilson and Neff actually reach a momentary rapport with the werewolves, who come forth more boldly than in the novel. Their urgency is generated by the modern destruction of their ecological environment. Though the film is an effective and witty thriller, it displeased Strieber, whose works are almost without humor. While Strieber is reputed to have a highly developed sense of humor, it seems to be an emotion his characters can ill afford as they move into a universe of peril. Indeed, the grim atmosphere of his works may sometimes make his readers yearn for a bit of Stephen King's "regular guy" horseplay, but the somber ambiance does fit Strieber's determination to look beyond the ordinary consolations of life.

The Hunger (1981) enhances its author's dark vision by focusing on another Gothic trope. Without ever using the word *vampire*, Strieber creates one of the most memorable vampires in literature in Miriam Blaylock. Millennia-old, Miriam combines the cunning, strength, and sensory superiority of the Wolfen with an angelic appearance. Humanoid, she can pass among people unnoticed—a fortunate circumstance since, like the werewolves, she uses people as sustenance by taking their blood (rather than their flesh). Unlike the Wolfen, however, Miriam is "a member of a failed species"—almost the last of her kind.[9] Without the community of a living tribe, she seeks out individual humans to assuage her loneliness, offering each companion an almost preternatural sexual ecstasy followed by the powerful promise of eternal life. That promise is false, belied by Miriam's own genetic structure—a cellular framework the human body can imitate for only a limited time. Uneasy with the lie, Miriam would like to find out if it can be turned into truth.

She sees a chance to do so in the work of Sarah Roberts, a doctor whose sleep research has brought her to the brink of discovering a way to stop the aging process. This work makes Sarah the prize in a struggle between Miriam and Tom Haver, the research director who is Sarah's lover. Appearing at the center as a superhuman stranger who seems to hold the key to immortality, Miriam deliberately enthralls Sarah. As for Tom, he tries to use both females in his climb to the top of the research center's administrative infrastructure. Tom is not a hypocrite, but everything in his petty world—love included—is political. When at last he realizes that the danger to Sarah is outside his control, he goes after her with nothing but his imperfect love as a weapon. Under Miriam's influence, Sarah kills him. The shock of doing so wakes her up enough to let her preserve her own soul by sacrificing her body.

To Miriam, such sacrifice is incomprehensible. Long ago, her own father died saving her, but even his sacrifice failed to imbue her with a sense of the value of unselfish love. Now, despite her attempts to return her companions' devotion, she remains truly devoted only to herself—a lone predator, but not a malicious one. Indeed, the book forces its readers to ponder the nature of predation itself. Vampires are, by definition, absolute predators; Strieber focuses all the sensuality, mystery, and horror of vampiric mythology on Miriam. With no enmity, indeed with a genuine fondness for the prey that gives her life, she kills because her kind must: "We are not evil," she says of her species; "we also are part of the justice of the earth." [10] In a Gothic universe, justice is not always kind.

That lack of kindness extends in all directions—exempting neither vampires nor humans. Miriam blames her tribe's demise on its inability to reconcile its feelings for humanity with its need for human blood—yet those feelings never stop her from feeding. Her species may, rather, have been doomed because it could never bond in the way of the Wolfen. Its empathy blunted by appetite, her tribe might have begun to die with her father's death. As a vampire, Miriam can never become part of anything larger than herself; she will always be alone. And though she tries to create the illusion of a familial bond with her companions, the connection always breaks, leaving her chosen not just in a hideous limbo between life and death, but also in a Gothic void between vampire and humankind.

Sarah's refusal to become a full-fledged vampire proves to Miriam that the two species will never become one. Reduced by that refusal to the agony that is Miriam's sole legacy, Sarah has the consolation that at least she is "a human being still." [11] And Miriam agrees, realizing that whatever she could offer this particular human "was not above one such as Sarah, but beneath her." [12] The predator is still in power at the end of *The Hunger*, but the prey has won the game. When Tony Scott's stylish film (1983) reversed that ending by having a surprisingly soulless Sarah replace Miriam as vampire, it lost the point of the book and confirmed Sheila Benson's comment: as a movie, it was "absolutely beautiful. And dumb." [13]

For several years after *The Hunger*, Strieber continued to write novels about inhuman or ultrahuman intrusions in *Black Magic* (1982), *The Night Church* (1983), and *Catmagic* (1986). These novels explore, in turn, the political chaos created by government, church, and science. In each succeeding novel, this human-created chaos is exploited by strangers who more and more seem literally of supernatural origin. But in 1985, Strieber published something different—a short novel for adolescents entitled *Wolf of Shadows*. This novel naturalized the Wolfen back into wolves who willingly allow a mother and daughter to join their pack during the turmoil of a nuclear winter. Told without romance, the story is a romantic tale of a real symbiosis—the humans are willing to share canned foods the wolves cannot get into and the wolves are able to kill what little game remains for them all. Each species remains distinct, but together they form a union that has a better chance at survival than either wolf or human would alone. Despite its grim setting, *Wolf of Shadows* may be Strieber's most hopeful novel—a fable suggesting that the self and the other may yet become an organic whole.

It was also during these years that Strieber and James Kunetka coauthored *Warday: And the Journey Onward* (1984) and *Nature's End* (1986). Each is a novel about apocalypse, reached through a nuclear exchange in the first book and ecological damage in the second. A restrained but detailed look at the aftermath of a limited atomic war, *Warday*'s strangers are the Soviets who launch a preemptive strike against America. The evil, however, does not lie in any single nationality, but in the "hostile competitiveness and ideological obsession" [14] that went out of control both in the United States and the Soviet Union. Structured as a series of interviews and documents, this postmodern text uses its authors not just as narrators, but also as protagonists whose relatives supposedly died in the fictional blasts that decimated San Antonio (where both writers actually grew up). Thus, Kunetka speaks of losing his wife and mother in the blast, while Strieber counts forty-seven dead relatives (eventually to become forty-eight, since he also took a heavy dose of radiation on Warday). By blurring the line between authors and characters, Strieber and Kunetka effectively convey the immediacy of the nuclear issue. They also personalize it in a way that can be seen as solipsistic if not downright masochistic. At any rate, having shrunken the gap between his fiction and his life, Strieber was now ready to plunge his narrative persona into *Communion.*

Nothing about *Communion,* subtitled *A True Story,* is easy—not even its publishing history. Despite being a bestselling author, Strieber had to write *Communion* on speculation before submitting it to thirteen houses, ten of which—in his own words—"turned it down, flat. Many with contempt."[15] The remaining three wanted it badly, however, and Morrow won the bid with a million-dollar advance. What Morrow won was a work detailing the close, intimate encounters Strieber asserts he actually has had with the nonhuman strangers he calls "visitors." While many readers and some reviewers accepted the book at face value (it became Strieber's biggest seller to date), scores of journalists, unbelievers, critics, and comedians did not. Ed Conroy has traced the storm of skeptical reaction in his well-written inquiry, *Report on Communion.* At the eye of the storm, Strieber spent a year or so defending himself in hundreds of interviews. He then went on to write the screenplay for *Communion* (1989), but the dull, though faithful, movie that resulted did little to appease his critics. Although he has proclaimed indifference to the debate over his credibility and even his sanity, Strieber remains, in Conroy's words, "in an ongoing trial," one that may never reach a verdict.[16]

The irony of this trial is that it has obscured that which seems most crucial in Strieber's canon: not who the strangers are or whether they exist outside their minstrel's mind, but what they mean. In *Communion,* Strieber admits that he has no idea where the visitors come from. As possible origins he offers outer space, an unknown evolutionary track, another dimension, a different time, "from within us," a secondary effect of natural phenomena, or even the afterlife.[17] That he uses the phrase "from within us" as one possibility is significant because it connects the human imagination to the widest interpretation of reality. The imagination becomes not just the creative center of the human self, but also its conduit into any extrahuman others. Imagination becomes more important than logic in determining truth. "You are our chosen one," Strieber remembers the visitors telling him, chosen, perhaps, because of the vision he has as a writer.[18] Just as the Romantic poet Shelley referred to artists as the legislators of the world, so Strieber sees himself as a legislator of the universe—not a politician, but a shaper of human awareness.

Strieber also readily admits the resemblance between the characters in his fiction and the creatures in the works he labels nonfiction—between the strangers like the Wolfen and the visitors of *Communion*. What matters to him is not who came first (he is convinced the visitors did); what matters is the psychological affect the visitors brought Strieber: first fear (the book's original title was *Body Terror*), then an acceptance of their power and influence. This acceptance was so profound that it became a communion, "as wide as all the knowledge of both partners, as deep as their whole souls."[19] For a man whose fiction had always dealt with tension, this sort of Shelleyan fusion implied the potential for peace.

Strieber went on to write another book he classified as nonfiction: *Transformation* (1988), the sequel to *Communion*, expands its author's sense of the visitors into a kind of new-age acceptance of all extraordinary phenomena. He then ended his trilogy on the visitor theme with a work of overt fiction, *Majestic* (1989). A historical novel, it speculates on what might have happened in a government cover-up of a 1947 unidentified flying object (UFO) incident in New Mexico. In *Majestic*, Strieber reveals the same distrust and disgust with politics that he shows in *The Wolfen*, *The Hunger*, *Black Magic*, *Warday*—in all his books to one degree or another. Politics restrict both vision and action in Strieber's canon, confining humans to their own little domain and preventing them from observing the larger cosmos. Only by transforming the political self into a receptive self can humanity open up to the realities that lie beyond our narrow interests.

However desirable such transformation may be in the visitor books, Strieber's work both before and after the *Communion* cycle suggests that it is also dangerous; the realities it reveals may be Gothic rather than romantic. Whatever the status of his personal tranquillity, Strieber's recent fiction remains ambivalent in its attitude toward transformation. *Billy* (1990) features a serial child-killer who kidnaps the twelve-year-old son of a middle-class family in Iowa. Barton Royal is a human stranger—

a psychopath who steals Billy Neary for the express purpose of making the child his son and molding his personality. But if Barton imagines himself a sculptor, the reshaping he actually seeks is not in Billy but in himself. Thinking of the boy, he writes, "Let me love you, serve you, become you," only to find himself startled and dismayed at what he has written.[20] With his pudgy body, repressed homosexuality, and underpaid job as a part-time clown, Barton echoes the recently executed killer, John Wayne Gacy. Like Gacy, he kills because he can neither admit what he is nor become anything different. When the police catch Barton, he commits suicide rather than expose his illusions to himself.

Thus, the relationship between Barton and Billy is unique in Strieber's canon. Miriam handpicks her companions in *The Hunger* and the visitors select their chosen one in *Communion*—but nowhere else does the chooser wish to be the chosen; nowhere else is the predator so obviously inferior to the prey. Billy, "one of those children who were so perfect that it seemed impossible that tragedy could ever reach them,"[21] is the novel's romantic hero—a golden boy who spends much of his time trying to recreate the music of a bird that sings outside his window. This Keatsian empathy is the hallmark of Billy's character: it allows him to play along with Barton's games, all the while knowing they will lead to torture and death. It lets him sense his brothers—the fourteen boys whose bodies have been stuffed into trash bags in Barton's basement. It even permits him to feel joy in the natural cycle of life that he is able to return to at the story's conclusion. One review called this conclusion "an oddly upbeat finale that rings not quite true,"[22] but it is the higher truth as represented by Billy. That truth is denied, though, to the fourteen earlier victims—some of whom end buried without names. *Billy* tries hard to establish a universe where the romantic triumphs, but there is a Gothic echo throughout the book that never dies away.

The Wild (1991) lacks the narrative strength of Strieber's best fiction, but it does serve as the apotheosis of his fascination with lycanthropy. Since *The Wolfen*, Strieber has been obsessed with wolves—a species he sees as a positive contrast to humankind. Unlike people, who ignore or abuse their environment, wolves reach out with their extended senses to the earth and to the universe at large with both rapture and respect. In *The Wild*, Bob Duke is called by wolves until he literally shapeshifts into one—thus bringing the species the intelligence it will need to guard what is left of the wilderness against human folly. At its core, *The Wild* is Kafka (unsurprisingly, Strieber's favorite author), influenced by the post-visitors *mentalité* so that metamorphosis is given meaning and purpose. It reads like a metaphor of the experience in and reaction to *Communion;* it reads like wish fulfillment.

Unholy Fire (1992) reverts to its author's pre-visitors sense of the Gothic peril inherent in the universe. The story of two priests involved in the investigation of a series of murders in their church, *Unholy Fire* is not a particularly original tale. Its revelation that one of the priests is possessed by a demon is standard Gothic fare. In *Unholy Fire*, however, the emphasis is not on the possession per se, but rather on the details of the priestly life that leave it open to possession. The book exposes the dogmatic restrictions that label physical contact a sin and then turn sin into catastrophe by hiding it within the soul until the soul bursts with guilt—a husk to be taken by whatever hellspawn happens by.

A lapsed Catholic, Strieber still reflects in his work a fascination with the expansive ritual of the church, but his own theology also encompasses both Zen and Wicca. What he wants from his religion is a Shelleyan reconciliation of humankind with strangers, self with other, and earth with universe. Thus, in *Transformation*, Strieber says that rather than reject the negative, "We must learn to walk the razor's edge between fear and ecstasy—in other words, to begin finally to seek the full flowering and potential of our humanity." [23] In *Unholy Fire*, Father John Rafferty is able to walk that edge; Father Frank Bayley cannot maintain his balance and so is swallowed by the demon, who uses him to recreate the uncontrolled cruelty of the church at its worst—the *auto-da-fé* fires of the Inquisition.

Those fires are stoked by Maria Julien, a beautiful woman who has seduced Frank and is about to seduce John. A kind of Mary Magdalen who believes in "the transformative value of sexual ecstasy," [24] Maria is determined to save the priests from hell—which she defines as "the discovery that you've missed your life." [25] Without being godly herself, she offers her clergy "a grace of woman," [26] but only John can admit his love for her. The politically minded Frank hides his love, thereby reducing it to furtive lust. Maria envisions herself as the stranger who will widen the horizons of these priests, but her own perspective is too narrow for her to comprehend the horror she has unleashed. Not knowing that Frank already carries the undeserved guilt of childhood molestation, she unwittingly pushes him toward the demonic other whose first victim she becomes. Like *The Hunger*, *Unholy Fire* suggests that those who do not grasp the full import of transformation may suffer awful consequences. Frank and Maria succumb to forces they only partially understand, leaving John—in another of Strieber's Pyrrhic victories—a better priest for having cherished both lost souls.

The margin of victory is even slimmer in *The Forbidden Zone* (1993). Dedicated to H. P. Lovecraft, this novel of absolute horror plays off Lovecraft's and Strieber's apparent beliefs in both alien existence and essential fear. It also adheres to Lovecraft's demand that the true weird tale present "a malign and particular suspension or defeat of those fixed laws of Nature which are our only safeguard against the assaults of chaos and the daemons of unplumbed space."[27] That safeguard is suspended by physicist Brian Kelly, whose work inadvertently opens the forbidden zone—the door between two phases of existence—so that a race of giant, intelligent insectoids can break out of their own time of famine and into today's world of plenty. The strangers here are uncontrolled predators and malignant monsters who seem like travesties of both the old gods and the visitors. Like cancer cells, the insectoids are lethal invaders whose existence depends on the destruction of their hosts.

Only one invader actually makes it through the door, but its predations are particularly repulsive: paralyzing its terrified victims with artificially induced orgasms, the invader then transforms them into a caricature of its own race—into drones modeled in hatred. Not just people, but all of nature is susceptible to this evil transformation—the Gothic nightmare made organic flesh. Amid forests oozing decay and machinery that becomes bestial, the population of two towns is seduced and decimated. Men and women are lost by a common weakness: the inability to imagine—much less resist—something so foreign as an invasion of other-dimensional evil. As the nexus between humanity and monstrosity, the forbidden zone becomes a metaphor for that area of darkness within the human soul that leaves it vulnerable to corruption.

What defeats the invasion is a single family—Brian Kelly's family—aware enough of evil to fight it despite their fear, and loving enough to withstand its temptation. Led by the Wordsworthian wisdom of their newborn infant, the Kellys manage to close the door on something worse than hell. But their romantic sensibility is the exception in humanity. The rule is the lack of discernment that leads to the death of most of their neighbors. The victory the Kellys win is real, but its implications are ominous: most of humanity simply cannot walk that razor's edge above a Gothic void.

Strieber believes that he can walk the edge—saying his visitor experience has taken away his fear and left him not just happy, but "incredibly empowered."[28] By accepting the notoriety and defamation that resulted from the *Communion* controversy, he has offered his experience to the world at large. In so doing, he has stayed true to his romantic belief that heightened perception opens up reality. Yet he remains "a lone wolf, skirting the edges of society" by identifying with an animal some associate with the "mercurial archetype of the 'Trickster.' "[29] His work—before and after the visitors—bears out this contradiction: while it does continually allow the human spirit to blossom by perceiving a higher reality, it also suggests that the vast majority of people will always be blind and that the higher reality the few may find is not always benign. The endless argument over just how much a prankster Strieber really is remains pointless. Like Keats's Adam, Whitley Strieber's truth is of the imagination. But like Byron, his is the Gothic imagination that sees more than the eyes can see and, sometimes, more than the heart can bear.

Notes

1. Gary Richard Thompson, ed., *The Gothic Imagination* (Pullman: Washington State University Press, 1974) 3.

2. Douglas E. Winter, "Whitley Strieber," *Faces of Fear* (New York: Berkeley, 1985) 193.

3. Ed Conroy, *Report on Communion* (New York: Morrow, 1989) 103.

4. Hoxie Neale Fairchild, *The Romantic Quest* (1931; New York: Russell & Russell, 1965) 370.

5. Winter, 198–99.

6. Whitley Strieber, *The Wolfen* (New York: Morrow, 1978) 154.

7. Barbara A. Bannon, rev. of *The Wolfen. Publishers Weekly* 3 July 1978: 61.

8. Strieber, *Wolfen* 154.

9. Whitley Strieber, *The Hunger* (New York: Morrow, 1981) 247.

10. Strieber, *Hunger* 67.

11. Strieber, *Hunger* 317.

12. Strieber, *Hunger* 319.

13. Sheila Benson, rev. of *The Hunger. Los Angeles Times* 30 April 1983: Calendar 6.

14. Whitley Strieber and James W. Kunetka, *Warday: And the Journey Onward* (New York: Holt, Rinehart, and Winston, 1984) 138.

15. Stanley Winter, "Beyond *Communion:* A Conversation with Whitley Strieber," *Twilight Zone* April 1988: 24.

16. Conroy, 345.

17. Whitley Strieber, *Communion* (New York: Beech Tree-Morrow, 1987) 223–24.

18. Strieber, *Communion* 83.

19. Strieber, *Communion* 280.

20. Whitley Strieber, *Billy* (New York: Putnam, 1990) 16.

21. Strieber, *Billy* 104.

22. Sybil Steinberg, rev. of *Billy, Publishers Weekly* 15 June 1990: 56.

23. Whitley Strieber, *Transformation* (New York: Beech Tree-Morrow, 1988) 242–43.

24. Whitley Strieber, *Unholy Fire* (New York: Dutton, 1992) 24.

25. Strieber, *Unholy Fire* 26.

26. Strieber, *Unholy Fire* 327.

27. Howard Phillips [H. P.] Lovecraft, *Supernatural Horror in Literature* (New York: Ben Abramson, 1945; New York: Dover, 1973) 15.

28. Winter, 87.

29. Conroy, 115.

8

Culture in
the Hall of Mirrors
Film and Fiction and Fiction and Film

Michael J. Collins

Over a hundred years before the horror boom of the past two decades began, fiction had already begun to assimilate and influence the
increasingly image-based popular culture of its time. The so-called
penny dreadfuls of the late Victorian age featured thrilling engravings
on their covers that were aimed primarily at capturing the attention of
prospective buyers and secondarily at illustrating some vital scene from
the story. Of course, the beginnings of narrative itself were visual—the
Paleolithic cave paintings of Lascaux and Font-de-Gaume served not
only as good-luck charms but also as stories of hunting prowess. The art
of Africa's Tassili n'Ajjer, dating back to 4000 B.C., includes gruesomely
fanciful caricatures; the 1000 B.C. Egyptian New Kingdom's papyri included irreverent secular works following narrative, in addition to holy,
trajectories. We also find alarming and occasionally horrific images employed in the service of storytelling in ancient Greek friezes; on Roman
reliefs; and in medieval incunabula, tapestries, and triptychs.

Throughout these early examples of visual narrative, horror has
lurked in various forms. From the plague-era recurrence of death iconog-
raphy to the post-Renaissance traditions of the *memento mori* and *vanitas*,
from the plastered skulls of the Neolithic to the grotesque African and
Native American/Eskimo carved war and ceremonial helmets, narrative
and its contemporary ancillary, fiction, have shown a perpetual concern
with the macabre. Horror's impact, no matter what the medium, depends largely upon imagery, whether pictorial (the art of Goya) or
descriptive (the vivid prose of Stephen King).

By the time Horace Walpole wrote the prototypical Gothic horror novel *The Castle of Otranto* in 1764, he had a rich tradition of fearsome imagery upon which to draw. The reading public seized upon the Gothic with such gleeful vigor that it was not long before Walpole's blueprints for the genre became permanently entrenched in the relatively recent form of the vernacular prose novel. Walpole inspired many imitators and developers of his style, among whom number Ann Radcliffe, William Beckford, and Matthew Lewis.

By the time penny dreadfuls like *Spring-Heel'd Jack* and *Varney the Vampyre; or, The Feast of Blood* turned up in the late nineteenth century, an eager audience awaited their empurpled chills. The industrial revolution had completely reshaped the structure of popular literature: increasingly sophisticated printing technologies created possibilities for widely distributed, affordable illustrated reading, and a completely revised class system created a literate audience with disposable income. As factories and mills sprouted in the cities, they attracted an influx of rural labor, in turn creating a demand for supervisors and managers, soon to become the middle class—intermediaries between the wealthy factory owners and the uneducated laborers. These midlevel workers, pockets newly lined, were pleased to spend money on amusements more respectable than the burlesque (which, after all, anyone could enjoy regardless of literacy) and more exciting than the opera (which was prohibitively expensive and discouragingly hard to understand). Our present popular culture was born in the Victorian era, and elements of the whaleboned repression that characterized Victorian morality continue to wield considerable power in popular culture.

The penny dreadfuls, like much contemporary horror, thrived on events that exceeded the tightly limned boundaries of their age's rectitude. Stories of criminals real and imagined, illustrated with titillating lithographs of crimes and executions, competed with more fantastic tales of ghosts and vampires—and for those wishing a blend of crime and horror, creepily illustrated accounts of premature burial and unsavory exhumations with emphases ranging from Burke-and-Harey nastiness to Usheresque necrophilic romance were equally in evidence.

The Victorian era also saw a growing interest in mechanical amusements. Such optical toys as the Thaumatrope, the Phenakistoscope, and the Zoetrope (most of which were popular roughly between 1860 and 1890) have rightfully earned their place in the prehistory of film; these devices primarily used sequential cartoons in repeating cycles, flickering through slits in revolving discs or cylinders, to achieve the illusion of motion. Seldom employing narrative, many of these strips made use of the fantastic possibilities of their media to deal with decidedly eerie and grotesque subjects. A few examples of Zoetrope strips (the authorship of which seems untraceable) feature such comically disturbing events as a bearded man waving a club at an endless procession of devil figures which dart between his legs; a caricatured Chinese fisherman doing battle with an enormous, amply fanged sea serpent; and a huge, evil-looking insect pursuing a man. Printed originally in the unnaturally glowing hues of early chromolithography, these strips, when spun in their machine, arguably constitute some of the first horror movies.

Photography, even from its inception, encompassed the element of horror. Though its origin remains a mystery, a set of nineteenth-century photographic plates discovered during the razing in the mid-1970s of an old Parisian block includes the following unsigned note: "This is the work of my entire life. It's the way I've imagined hell. If I've seen it accurately, as the wretched reassure themselves, eternity will be sweet for them to endure." [1]

The photographs represent *La vie quotidienne chez Satan*, [daily life in Satan's domain] and depict meticulously produced ceramic tableaux. These Boschian images are populated with the skeletal damned involved in all manner of everyday sin—seducing one another, drinking, dissipating themselves with merry abandon in gambling dens and "des odalisques." Lest we feel unduly tempted by this postmortal Pleasure Island, we are also treated to such nasty sights as the damned employed in foundries, whipped, and tortured. The Victorian era's increasingly complex psychological relationship with technology, sexuality, and theology acted itself out across its cultural proscenium, developing ever greater affinity for the image.

As the century turned and film began its passage from novelty to cultural staple, horror quickly made its presence known on flickering nitrate. Such early spook shows as Melies' 1896 *Le Manoir du Diable* [The House of the Devil] and 1899 *Le Diable au Convent* [The Devil at the Convent] were conceived and scripted by Melies himself, but the film adaptation of horror fiction was around just as early. Melies adapted H. Rider Haggard's novel *She* to film under the title *La Danse du Feu* [The Dance of Fire] in 1899. Eleven years later J. Searle Dawley, directing for Edison's Vitagraph company, made the first screen adaptation of *Frankenstein* (Vitagraph laid more groundwork in American film than has been credited—the studio is responsible for the first mondo documentary, *The Electrocution of an Elephant*, as well as an early trip/dream film, *Dream of a Rarebit Fiend.*)

With the appearance of such adaptations, already long a staple of the stage, horror film and fiction began a dialogue of mutual aesthetic influence that grew continually more important as the cinema matured. The advent of the tie-in novel (an early example is the 1926 novel *Metropolis*, after Fritz Lang's film) signaled that film was not merely an outgrowth of drama and literature, but an active element in a rapidly evolving, vital culture.

A complete history of the interrelation between horror film and fiction would exceed by far the limitations of this essay, but a few brief examples prior to the contemporary period are worth noting. We are all aware of *Dracula* and *Frankenstein*, and Roger Corman's 1960s series of loose Poe adaptations (including *House of Usher* (1960), *The Pit and the Pendulum* (1961), and *The Premature Burial* (1962)) has also received ample documentation, in works from Michael Weldon's *Psychotronic Encyclopedia of Film* to Corman's own *How I Made Over 100 Movies in Hollywood (And Never Lost a Dime)*. The reverse influence is equally noteworthy: best-selling horror novelist Ramsey Campbell pseudonymously penned adaptations of such Universal favorites as *Dracula*, *Frankenstein*, and *The Wolf Man*, a situation which encapsulates the film/fiction crossover with paradoxical irony. An interesting and lesser-recalled tie-in series from Warren Publications (best known for their post-EC comics *Creepy* and *Eerie*) consisted of photo-comic magazine adaptations of the films *The Mole People* (1956), *The Curse of Frankenstein* (1957), *The Horror of Dracula* (1958), and *Horror of Party Beach* (1964). Long considered a form of dubious distinction at best, the photo-comic and its chubbier uncle, the fotonovel, exemplify the rapidly dissolving boundaries between the various popular forms of narrative: novels, plays, film, comics, and photography have grown less and less distinct from one another since the industrial revolution.

The contemporary period, for the purpose of this essay, may be considered as having begun with the release of Ira Levin's 1967 novel *Rosemary's Baby*. Though important, influential horror literature certainly preceded Levin's novel, *Rosemary's Baby* has an aggressively visual prose style and, equally important, a genuinely cinematic structure. Its relative brevity (245 pages in its original hardcover release) and its use of tight, well-defined scenes which build in concise, spartan sequence give the novel an unmistakable air of the feature film. Levin's use of compressed-time transitions frequently takes the form of cinematic scene-linkage sequences—brief vignettes having the same effect as time-passage transitions in film:

> She bought cotton balls and cotton swabs and talcum powder and baby lotion; engaged a diaper service and rearranged the baby's clothing in the bureau drawers. She ordered the announcements— Guy would phone in the name and date later—and addressed and stamped a boxful of small ivory envelopes. She read a book called *Summerhill* that presented a seemingly irrefutable case for permissive child-rearing, and discussed it at Sardi's East with Elise and Joan, their treat.[2]

Levin's novel uses inherently cinematic techniques. Opening with the prose equivalent of an establishing shot, the novel thrusts us immediately into the story, realizing characters through action and physical description more than through traditionally literary introspection. Importantly, much of the story and character development emerges through dialogue: Levin has the ear of a playwright and uses distinctive phrasing and meter with such understated skill that, as in film, we come to know characters through their speech. Without stooping to the labored phonetic apostrophizing that passes in some work as dialect, Levin's writing propels story and character sensually more than psychologically. One hears and sees this novel rather than thinks it.

By weaving together the diverse threads of its current culture (a papal visit; a concurrent decline in traditional Christianity and increase in spiritual experimentation) and braiding into it concerns over Christian ideas of good and evil, Levin's novel achieves the status to which many films aspire—a potent blend of present-tense immediacy with issues of perennial concern. Where slightly earlier novels of similar depth and deftness (John Wyndham's 1957 *The Midwich Cuckoos*, for example) work best within the sedately paced, omniscient literary tradition, Levin's novel introduced the pacing, development, and structure of film to the work of literature. This diffusion of stylistic influence was hardly a new thing. But Levin's novel earned its popularity *as literature*; this horror novel catalyzed the genre's exploding popularity over the coming years, a popularity originally rooted, as are most cultural booms, in trendsetting respectability.

Levin's novel, and Roman Polanski's William Castle-produced adaptation of 1968, began the burgeoning popularity of horror as more-or-less mainstream entertainment. To the public of the late 1960s, horror's chief representatives were the American-International Pictures released in epic quantity a few years earlier and the EC scandal of the 1950s, in which professional concerned citizen Dr. Fredric Wertham successfully managed to plant a specious hysteria in the heads of concerned parents over the ostensibly deleterious effects of horror comics. The success of Levin's novel, and Roman Polanski's excellent film adaptation, began horror's ever-tenuous flirtation with critical acceptance on its own terms, and the immense critical and popular success of the film adaptation accorded horror, at least for a few precious years, the perceived status of serious art.

The next major horror novel of the era was William Peter Blatty's *The Exorcist* (1971). Similarly concerned with classic ideas of evil, Blatty's novel, like Levin's, uses sharp, graphic imagery for its punchier scenes, connected by rather more labored stretches of character probing. Blatty used distinctive, ornamental prose for his character development, contrasting it violently with clear, declarative passages detailing the scare scenes. The cinematic form here is augmented by pugnaciously presented events, echoing the film genre's growing use of like-mindedly trenchant moments: "Karras was suddenly dodging a projectile stream of vomit, leaping out of his chair. It caught a portion of his sweater and one of his hands. His face now colorless, the priest looked down at the bed. Regan cackled with glee. His hand dripped vomit onto the rug."[3]

Scenes like these were strong stuff in novels, and they would have been more so on screen. In 1971 the MPAA's ratings system was still new. Established in 1968, the *G, GP, R* and *X* system was a response to a growing tendency of both Hollywood and foreign films to flout the Production Code, the system of moral guidelines that had for decades governed film content and approach. Violence and nudity had arrived in force and showed no inclination to depart. Coincidental with the appearance of the *R* and *X* ratings (the latter of which had yet to be associated exclusively with sex) came the appearance of explicit violence in popular film. Gore-heavy movies had existed for quite a few years prior to the late 1960s: most notably, the later films of Dr. Herschell Gordon Lewis were gleefully blood-sodden exercises in cartoonish brutality (*Blood Feast* [1963], *Two Thousand Maniacs* [1964], and many others). But the tumultuous later 1960s saw unabashed mainstream admiration for films featuring bloody violence. Hammer films like *The Curse of Frankenstein* (1957), *Horror of Dracula* (1958), and *The Curse of the Werewolf* (1961), among many others—tame and ponderous as they may seem to a current eye—were occasionally vilified for their bloodiness. Films from outside the genre, too, had begun to feature bloodier acts: *Bonnie and Clyde* (1967), *The Wild Bunch* (1968), and *Easy Rider* (1969), though not horror films, were all successful, popular, and rather bloody films. The all-too-real bloodshed that aired on nightly news programs showing the carnage of Vietnam had raised the tolerance of viewers, and moviegoers' stronger stomachs and desire for antidotally unreal violence caused Hollywood to rise to the challenge.

Horror's major contribution to the growing cinematic plasma center, of course, was George A. Romero's unrated 1968 *Night of the Living Dead*. A controversial film in a controversial time, Romero's story of refugees fortifying a farmhouse against a flesh-eating-zombie attack inspired as much discussion as it did condemnation. Like *Rosemary's Baby* the same year, it ladled generous portions of literal and allegorical references to its era. The Coopers' zombie-bitten daughter, who eventually kills her mother with a trowel, is one of the first in what would become a series of evil-kid characters—heady stuff for a culture bitterly divided between generations. Ben, the pragmatic black hero, struggles through the long night only to die at the hands of the roving militia, which has mistaken him for a zombie—a bleak ending well suited to a cynical and disintegrating society. *Night of the Living Dead* added much fuel to the late 1960s' signature inferno of controversy.

Most important are the effect these films had upon culture and the effect these events had upon the literary subset of culture. The most visible, and visual, instance of this heightening mayhem came in scenes like the above example from *The Exorcist*. Literary horror and film horror exceeded themselves apace: where *Rosemary's Baby* echoed the form of horror film, *The Exorcist* echoed the content. Two years later, in 1973, William Friedkin's film adaptation once again redefined the genre's limits.

Before 1973 film horror faced practical as well as aesthetic boundaries. Beyond social checks governing what one could get away with on-screen (an aesthetic boundary), filmmakers also had to work around the fact that some effects simply could not be achieved convincingly. The early 1960s gore films of Herschell Gordon Lewis depended upon large amounts of stage blood, both to shock and to conceal the phony gutbags attached to his tolerant actors. In Hitchcock's celebrated shower montage from *Psycho*, he adapts standard stagecraft techniques of misdirection to create an impression, rather than a depiction, of brutality. It was not until the later 1960s that small explosive charges would come into use beneath blood bags (devices known as squibs) to simulate gunshot wounds (the end of *The Wild Bunch* positively fountains with them), and it was not until 1973 and *The Exorcist* that the boundaries of aesthetic and technical possibility would allow straightforward, convincing images of a twelve-year-old girl's head rotating 360 degrees or of her vomiting onto a priest. The development of these techniques had far-reaching impact. Where the imagery of horror writing had previously been capable of flights impossible to convincingly duplicate cinematically, film suddenly caught up with literature, and the stakes climbed higher.

One year after the release of *The Exorcist,* Stephen King published *Carrie.* King's writings, moving through his succeeding (and successful) works like *'Salem's Lot* (1975), *The Shining* (1977), *The Dead Zone* (1979), and onward, reflect his many influences, among which film figures prominently. In his superb study of the genre, *Danse Macabre,* King accords at least as much attention to film as to fiction, and his own writing draws much from the form, style, and technique of film. King's suspense-building technique of switching from event to event at climactic, cliff-hanging moments recalls the cinematic technique of crosscutting. Crosscutting, or parallel editing, found its first mature expression in D. W. Griffith's seminally inventive (and politically reactionary) 1915 film *The Birth of a Nation.* Alternating between two simultaneous events, crosscutting plays upon a viewer's desire for closure to intensify excitement—King's proficiency in suspenseful plotting and his frequently exquisite sense of pacing are as indebted to film as is his willingness to feature sharply limned descriptive passages detailing all manner of horrific material.

The horror boom of the 1970s begat the careers of many writers and filmmakers (most of these writers are chronicled in this book, and the filmmakers include John Carpenter, Tobe Hooper, Wes Craven, and David Cronenberg), and like any popular event with money connected to it, it inspired quick-money bandwagon jumpers. Mediocre writers like Clare McNally, V. C. Andrews, and Graham Masterton met a public more voracious than discerning. Horror film faced a similar situation—the success of *The Exorcist* and *Carrie* inspired dozens of imitators, some good *(The Omen, The Fury),* most not. Once again, though, the important popular success of both novel and film created a trend which gradually evolved into a subgenre, absorbed by both film and literature.

The system of aesthetic exchange between prose and screen—not restricted to horror but most visible there—grew more cyclical and less linear with each successive adaptation and tie-in. Novels spawn films, films spawn tie-ins, one form augments popular interest in the other. A best-selling novel (*Carrie*, for example) can become a successful film, which in turn revives interest in the novel, which, when reread, inspires a reader to watch the film again. The inclusion of movie stills in postfilm reissues of paperbacks (such as *Christine*) is significant to the change in a reader's relationship to both film and book. Writing, no matter how precise, may elicit in every reader a different response. With the addition of photo sections, however, readers' experiences of a novel become more unified, at least in connection to the events and characters represented in the stills.

The advent of the so-called slasher film in the late 1970s inspired a corresponding increase in bloody literary imagery. Slasher films are generally bloody thrillers featuring a series of creatively murdered teenagers whose deaths are usually preceded by sex, drugs, and rock and roll. These films, amply dissected by Vera Dika in *The Slasher Film* and Carol Clover in *Men, Women, and Chainsaws*, were immensely popular with adolescent audiences in the early 1980s. Novelizations proliferated and even now occasionally resurface despite their apparently ephemeral purposes (one such novel is Dean R. Koontz's 1994 paperback best-seller *The Funhouse*, originally released under the pseudonym Owen West to tie in with the 1981 Tobe Hooper effort). Relatively few slasher films were adapted from novels, but outside that subgenre, horror films continued to develop from novels. Many of horror's best literary efforts inspired films which ended up stunning duds—Straub's *Ghost Story*, a novel which deftly blends the genre's many historical strains, including the atmospheric as well as the graphic, became director John Irvin's sketchy failure.

Irvin's film is not the only misadapted horror film of the era, but its failure suggests much when compared to the frigid perfection of Stanley Kubrick's film version of King's novel *The Shining*. Both novels are fairly long: Straub's, in paperback, is 567 pages; King's is 447. The difference lies in the approach the films take to their source materials, which are themselves differently suited to film.

Novels and films are obviously different forms and demand different avenues of approach. What makes Irvin's film a failure is not simply his film's panicky condensing of 567 pages into 110 minutes, it is also the fact that Irvin or his screenwriter (Lawrence D. Cohen) did not adapt the novel to film but merely illustrated some of its highlights. One needs to have read the book to decipher the film: characters have little motivation and no history, and events are similarly muddled. It seems to have selected only the most superficial of the novel's many delicately woven story lines. In contrast, Kubrick, whose cold mastery of the medium has produced a body of superlative films, distills the events and characters of King's novel and augments them with skill—Kubrick transforms the characters, events, and settings of the novel into elements better suited to film, whereas Irvin attempts to retain elements from the novel which do not work as film (characters from the book appear in the film with no explanation of their connection to the plot). Successful transformation of print to film demands an understanding of both. Irvin is a more than competent director, Cohen a skilled screenwriter, but neither is an especially gifted reader. Kubrick's skills function equally well across the postmodern zone of intertextuality in its truest sense—a well-considered understanding of the connections between various media and discourses.

Another contribution of *The Shining* to the genre is its blend of escalating fear and nasty wit; a blend which would soon become associated with "splatterpunk." It was in the mid-1980s that the term *splatterpunk* began to appear in fanzines and conventions. Though no firm definition of the term has ever existed, it soon became a convenient label for a changing approach to horror writing. Such authors as Clive Barker, Richard Christian Matheson, John Skipp, Craig Spector and many others used vividly descriptive language and characterization through action rather than introspection to craft gleefully violent stories in which gore figures prominently. Splatterpunk may have had its literary roots in *Rosemary's Baby* or *The Exorcist*, but it has done well in film.

David J. Schow, credited with coining the term *splatterpunk*, was also, not coincidentally, the editor of the 1988 anthology *Silver Scream*, a collection of short stories confronting the complex influence of cinema in our culture. Schow, along with several of the other writers associated with the subgenre, implements his talents as a screenwriter as well as a prose stylist—Schow brought these converging influences into focus by having Tobe Hooper (director of *The Texas Chain Saw Massacre* [1974], *Eaten Alive* [1976], *Poltergeist* [1982], and other films of progressively decreasing quality) write the anthology's introduction, which appears in the form of a screenplay.

Stories in *Silver Scream* confront the gamut of cinematic horrors. Of particular significance are stories such as Steven R. Boyett's "The Answer Tree" and Mark Arnold's "Pilgrims to the Cathedral," which use the psychological and physical act of watching movies as their source material. The stories in this book are not tie-ins; they are something even more meaningful—fiction which has adapted not only its style, but its entire understanding of culture, from cinema.

For some critics the notion that splatterpunk was cinematic rather than literary horror was an indictment of its craft. Cinematic horror, the sentiment ran, depended upon superficial shocks, nose-rubbing glee in visceral gore, and an overall dedication to high-gloss veneer at the expense of real substance. What this argument overlooks is the fact that cinema and prose have no essence—they are forms of expression, no more representative of any specific approach than paint not yet applied to canvas, clay awaiting the potter's hand. "Quiet horror" *is* cinematic in works like Tourneur's films of the 1940s (*Cat People*, *I Walked With A Zombie*, others). Film is a medium capable of just as broad a range of tone as prose, and it is a mistake to compare them without an appreciation of both.

A temptation in considering the splatterpunk agenda is to compare the stories to body-count slasher films. The stories began to appear just as the boom in slasher film began to wane, a fact possibly owing to the relative youth of splatterpunk authors, who were more likely to attend slasher films than their elders, and gore had become a familiar element in the movies, though not so much so in print. But the slasher films, in their most generic sense, are splatter without punk—they are form without force (at least, a lot of them are; note that a substantial number of slasher films—*Halloween* [1978], and its forebears *The Texas Chain Saw Massacre*, *Last House on the Left*, and the early canon of Dario Argento—are excellent, intelligent pieces of work). The basic formula of the slasher film privileged gore effects over character, story, and style. Hence, the cinematic comparison became an ignorant attempt at snobbishness.

The early 1980s saw dozens of slasher films, which began to evolve into something somewhat different with the release of 1984's *A Nightmare on Elm Street*. The film introduced a slasher-type villain, Freddy Krueger, in a surreal, malleable world in which rules of physics and rationality no longer applied. The same year saw the publication of Clive Barker's much-vaunted *Books of Blood*, a series of short-story collections which explore a similarly boundless world of graphic physiological terrors. Barker acknowledged his debt to film with "Son of Celluloid," a wildly inventive tale of a sentient tumor, metamorphosing endlessly into a series of movie stars, and he went on to become a screenwriter and director of respectable, if uneven, quality.

The *Nightmare* films began a steady drift toward self-parody, as Freddy (who became as familiar—and ultimately as tiresome—a figure in popular culture as any) became the world's cutest oneiric pedocidal maniac. Following a similar path were many splatterpunk stories, setting aside their *epater le bourgoisie* pluck in favor of precocious flash: any number of the stories collected in Paul Sammon's *Splatterpunks* will, with few exceptions, serve as examples.

But the cinematic strain grew ever more evident, perhaps reaching its clearest expression in Skipp and Spector's 1991 novel *The Bridge*. An ecological horror allegory concerning a toxic-waste monster, the novel brims with filmic technique, appropriating everything from *The Blob* (1958) to *The Toxic Avenger* (1985) and beyond. In addition to this overt influence, the authors inserted an advertisement in the back flyleaf pushing an actual soundtrack album for the novel, performed by the two authors. Calling their effort a soundtrack "for the movie in your mind," they leave no doubt as to their influences.

Film and fiction, along with comics, drama, painting, and music, have never been such disparate forms. As arts and crafts merged in the nineteenth century to meet the demands of a new consuming class, popular culture was born, and with it a new audience for horror. As horror developed, along with its culture, it recognized no boundaries of form: *Frankenstein,* beginning its existence as Mary Shelley's novel, became, as did Bram Stoker's *Dracula,* a play, a variety of movies, a figure in many pieces of music, and an icon instantly recognizable by nearly everyone.

What all this conclusively demonstrates is that horror is a perennial element of popular culture and, finally, that the boundaries of our culture are drawn by genre, not by form. As culture develops and technologies evolve, horror frequently operates at the forefront of formal innovation. As film was beginning, one of its first choices for material was horror literature, and as film matured, horror literature was one of the first literary genres to adapt its form to the influence of cinema. As electronic media proliferate, horror continues to explore their narrative potential long before other genres—romance, comedy, fantasy—take tentative steps toward timeliness. Horror, ultimately, acts as the voice of every successive generation, and tailors its approach accordingly. The differences between writing, film, and video fade steadily.

Notes

1. Jac Remise, *Diableries: La vie quotidienne chez Satan a la fin du 19e siecle* (Poitiers/Aubin: Ballard, 1978) 1. My translation.

2. Ira Levin, *Rosemary's Baby* (New York: Random House, 1967) 191.

3. William Peter Blatty, *The Exorcist* (New York: Harper & Row, 1971) 207.

Bibliography

Primary Source Material

This list, which emphasizes heavily American horror fiction published during the years 1988–1994, supplements the recommendations in appendixes to Stephen King's *Danse Macabre* (New York: Everest House, 1981), Douglas E. Winter's *Faces of Fear* (New York: Berkley, 1985), *Horror: 100 Best Books*, ed. by Stephen Jones and Kim Newman (New York: Carroll & Graf, 1988), and the excellent survey by Keith Neilson in chap. 4 of *Horror Literature: A Reader's Guide*, ed. by Neil Barron (New York: Garland, 1989).

Abe, Kobo. *The Face of Another.* New York: Knopf, 1966.

Ackroyd, Peter. *First Light.* New York: Viking, 1989.

Anker, Robert, ed. *Charles Beaumont: Selected Stories.* Arlington Heights: Dark Harvest, 1988.

Aycliffe, Jonathan. *Naomi's Room.* London: HarperCollins, 1991. New York: Harper Paperbacks, 1992.

Bachman, Richard [Stephen King]. *Rage.* New York: NAL, 1977.

———. *The Running Man.* New York: NAL, 1982.

Baker, Scott. *Webs.* New York: Tor, 1989.

Barker, Clive. *Books of Blood,* 6 vols. London: Sphere, 1984–1985.

Barry, Jonathan, with Whitley Streiber, *Catmagic.* New York: Tor, 1986.

Birnbaum, Alfred, ed. *Monkey Brain Sushi: New Tastes in Japanese Fiction.* New York: Kodansha International, 1991.

Blatty, William Peter. *Which Way to Mecca, Jack?* New York: Bernard Geis, 1960.

———. *John Goldfarb, Please Come Home!* New York: Doubleday, 1963.

———. *I, Billy Shakespeare.* New York: Doubleday, 1965.

———. *Twinkle, Twinkle "Killer" Kane.* New York: Doubleday, 1967.

———. *The Exorcist.* New York: Harper & Row, 1971.

———. *I'll Tell Them I Remember You.* New York: Norton, 1973.

———. *The Ninth Configuration.* New York: Harper & Row, 1978.

———. *Legion.* New York: Simon & Schuster, 1983.

Bloch, Robert. *Psycho.* New York: Simon & Schuster, 1959.

———. "Time Wounds All Heels." In *Fantastic Adventures* (April 1942).

Blumlein, Michael. *The Brains of Rats.* Los Angeles: Scream/Press, 1989.

Blunt, Giles. *Cold Eye.* New York: Morrow, 1990.

Bradfield, Scott. *Dream of the Wolf.* New York: Knopf, 1990.

Brite, Poppy Z. *Lost Souls*. New York: Delacorte, 1992.

Butler, Jack. *Nightshade*. New York: Atlantic Monthly Press, 1989.

Cadigan, Pat. *Patterns*. Kansas City: Ursus, 1989.

Cadnum, Michael. *Nightlight*. New York: St. Martin's Press, 1989.

————. *Sleepwalker*. New York: St. Martin's Press, 1990.

Cady, Jack. *The Sons of Noah and Other Stories*. Seattle: Broken Moon Press, 1992.

Campbell, Ramsey. *The Face that Must Die*. London: Wyndham/Star, 1979. Rev. ed., Santa Cruz, Calif.: Scream Press, 1983.

————. *Midnight Sun*. New York: Tor; London: Macdonald, 1990.

————. *The Influence*. London: Macmillan, 1988. New York: Tor, 1991.

————. *The Count of Eleven*. London: Macdonald, 1991. New York: Tor, 1992.

Carrére, Emmanual. *Gothic Romance*. New York: Scribners, 1990.

Carroll, Jonathan. *A Child Across the Sky*. London: Century, 1989. New York: Doubleday, 1990.

Chappell, Fred. *More Shapes Than One*. New York: St. Martin's Press, 1991.

Colchie, Thomas, ed. *A Hammock Beneath the Mangoes*. New York: Dutton, 1991.

Collins, Nancy A. *Tempter*. New York: Onyx, 1990.

Cooper, Dennis. *Frisk*. New York: Grove, Weidenfeld, 1991.

Cramer, Kathryn, ed. *Walls of Fear*. New York: Morrow, 1990.

Cramer, Kathryn, and Peter D. Pautz, eds. *The Architecture of Fear*. New York: Arbor House, 1987.

Daniels, Les. *No Blood Spilled*. New York: Tor, 1990.

Dark, Larry, ed. *The Literary Ghost*. New York: Atlantic Monthly Press, 1991.

Datlow, Ellen, ed. *Alien Sex*. New York: Dutton, 1990.

————, ed. *Blood Is Not Enough*. New York: Morrow, 1990.

————, ed. *A Whisper of Blood*. New York: Morrow, 1991.

————, and Terri Windling, eds. *The Year's Best Fantasy and Horror: Seventh Annual Collection*. New York: St. Martins Press, 1994.

Denton, Bradley. *Blackburn*. New York: St. Martins Press, 1993.

Disch, Thomas M. *The Businessman: A Tale of Terror*. New York: Harper Row, 1984.

————. *The M.D.: A Horror Story*. New York: Knopf, 1991.

Ellis, Bret Easton. *American Psycho*. New York: Viking, 1991.

Elrod, P. N. *Blood Lust: The Vampire Files I*. New York: Ace, 1990.

Etchison, Dennis. *The Dark Country*. Sacramento: Scream Press, 1982.

————. *Red Dreams*. Sacramento: Scream Press, 1984.

————. *Darkside*. New York: Charter, 1986.

————. *The Blood Kiss*. Los Angeles: Scream Press, 1988.

————, ed. *MetaHorror*. New York: Dell Abyss, 1992.

Fowler, Christopher. *Rune: A Novel of Urban Horror*. London: Century, 1990. New York: Ballantine, 1991.

Gallagher, Stephen. *Valley of Lights*. London: New English Library, 1987.

Gannett, Lewis. *The Living One*. New York: Random House, 1993.

Garton, Ray. *Live Girls.* New York: Pocket, 1987.

Grant, Charles L., *Greystone Bay.* New York: Tor, 1985.

————. ed. *Final Shadows.* New York: Doubleday, 1991.

Gregory, Stephen. *The Woodwitch.* New York: St. Martin's Press, 1989.

Harris, Allan Lee. *Deliver Us from Evil.* New York: Bantam, 1988.

Harris, Thomas. *Black Sunday.* New York: Putnam, 1975.

————. *Red Dragon.* New York: New American Library, 1981.

————. *The Silence of the Lambs.* New York: St. Martin's Press, 1988.

Hartwell, David G., ed. *The Dark Descent.* New York: Tor, 1987.

————, ed. *The Foundations of Fear.* New York: Tor, 1992.

Hawthorne, Nathaniel. *Mosses from an Old Manse.* New York and London: Wiley and Putnam, 1846.

Heidish, Marcy. *The Torching.* New York: Simon & Schuster, 1992.

Heller, Joseph. *Catch-22.* New York: Simon & Schuster, 1961.

Ingalls, Rachel. *The End of Tragedy.* New York: Simon & Schuster, 1987.

Jeter, K. W. *The Night Man.* New York: Onyx-NAL, 1990.

Kesey, Ken. *One Flew over the Cuckoo's Nest.* New York: Viking, 1962.

King, Stephen. *Carrie.* Garden City: Doubleday, 1974.

————. *'Salem's Lot.* New York: Signet, 1976.

————. *The Shining.* New York: Signet, 1978.

————. *The Stand.* Garden City: Doubleday, 1978. Rev. ed., Garden City: Doubleday, 1990.

————. *The Dead Zone.* New York: Viking, 1979.

————. *Firestarter.* New York: Viking, 1980.

————. *Cujo.* New York: Viking, 1981.

————. "The Body." *Different Seasons.* New York: Viking, 1982.

————. *Christine.* New York: Viking, 1983.

————. *Pet Sematary.* Garden City: Doubleday, 1983.

————. *Cycle of the Werewolf.* New York: NAL, 1984.

————. *The Long Walk. The Bachman Books: Four Early Novels by Stephen King.* New York: NAL, 1985.

————. *It.* New York: Viking, 1986.

————. *Misery.* New York: Viking, 1987.

————. *Needful Things.* New York: Viking, 1987.

————. *The Tommyknockers.* New York: Putnam, 1987.

————. *The Dark Half.* New York: Viking, 1989.

————. *Four Past Midnight.* New York: Viking, 1990.

————. *Gerald's Game.* New York: Viking, 1992.

————. *Dolores Claiborne.* New York: Viking, 1993.

————. *Insomnia.* New York: Viking, 1994.

King, Stephen, and Peter Straub. *The Talisman.* New York: Viking; New York: Putnam, 1984.

Klein, T. E. D. *The Ceremonies.* New York: Viking, 1984.

Koja, Kathe. *The Cipher.* New York: Dell Abyss, 1991.

———. *Bad Brains*. New York: Dell Abyss, 1992.

Koontz, Dean. *Whispers*. New York: Putnam, 1980.

———. *Lightning*. New York: Putnam, 1988.

———. *The Bad Place*. New York: Putnam, 1988.

———. *Midnight*. New York: Putnam, 1989.

———. *Mr. Murder*. New York: Putnam, 1994.

Lansdale, Joe R. *The Nightrunners*. Arlington Heights: Dark Harvest, 1987.

Lessing, Doris. *The Fifth Child*. New York: Viking, 1988.

Levin, Ira. *Rosemary's Baby*. New York: Random House, 1967.

Ligotti, Thomas. *Songs of a Dead Drummer*. New York: Carroll & Graf, 1989.

———. *Grimscribe: His Life and Works*. New York: Carroll & Graf, 1991.

Martin, George R. R. *The Armageddon Rag*. New York: Poseidon, 1984.

Martin, Valerie. *Mary Reilly*. New York: Doubleday, 1990.

Matheson, Richard. *I Am Legend*. New York: Fawcett, 1954.

———. *Scars and Other Distinguishing Marks*. Los Angeles: Scream/Press, 1987.

———. *The Collected Stories of Richard Matheson*. Los Angeles: Scream/Press, 1989.

———. *Created By*. New York: Bantam, 1993.

McAllister, Bruce. *Dream Baby*. New York: Tor, 1991.

McCammon, Robert R. *Swan Song*. New York: Pocket Books, 1987.

———. *Mine*. New York: Pocket, 1990.

McDowell, Michael. *Blackwater*. New York: Avon, 1983.

McEwan, Ian. *Black Dogs*. New York: Doubleday/Nan A. Talese, 1991.

McGrath, Patrick. *Blood and Water and Other Tales*. New York: Poseidon Press, 1988.

———. *The Grotesque*. New York: Poseidon Press, 1989.

———. *Spider*. New York: Poseidon Press, 1990.

———. *Dr. Haggard's Disease*. New York: Poseidon Press, 1993.

Monteleone, Thomas, ed. *Borderlands I*. New York: Avon, 1990.

Moore, Alan. *Watchmen*. New York: Warners, 1987.

Morrow, Bradford, and Patrick McGrath, eds. *The New Gothic: A Collection of Contemporary Gothic Fiction*. New York: Random House, 1991.

Newman, Kim. *The Night Mayor*. London: Simon & Schuster, 1989.

Night of the Living Dead. Dir. George Romero. Image Ten, 1968.

Nolan, William F., and Martin H. Greenburg, eds. *Urban Horrors*. Arlington Heights: Dark Harvest, 1990.

O'Neil, Timothy. *Shades of Gray*. New York: Viking, 1987.

Parkinson, T. L. *The Man Upstairs*. New York: Dutton, 1991.

Partridge, Norman. *Slippin' into Darkness*. Baltimore: CD Publications, 1994.

Prest, Thomas Prescott. *Varney the Vampire; or, The Feast of Blood*. N.p.: E. Lloyd, 1847.

Quinn, Daniel. *Dreamer*. New York: Tor, 1988.

Reeve-Steven, Garfield. *Dark Matter*. New York: Doubleday, 1990.

Rice, Anne. *Interview with the Vampire*. New York: Knopf, 1976.

————. *The Feast of All Saints*. New York: Simon & Schuster, 1979.
————. *The Vampire Lestat*. New York: Knopf, 1985.
————. *Cry to Heaven*. New York: Knopf, 1986.
————. *The Queen of the Damned*. New York: Knopf, 1988.
————. *The Mummy, or Ramses the Damned*. New York: Ballantine, 1989.
————. *The Witching Hour*. New York: Knopf, 1990.
————. *The Tale of the Body Thief*. New York: Knopf, 1992.
————. *Lasher*. New York: Knopf, 1993.
————. *Taltos: The Lives of the Mayfair Witches*. New York: Knopf, 1994.
Rickman, Phil. *Curfew*. 1993. Rpt. as *Crybbe*. New York: Putnam, 1994.
Rodgers, Alan. *Fire*. New York: Bantam, 1989.
Roszak, Theodore. *Flicker*. New York: Summit Books, 1991.
Salmonson, Jessica Amanda, ed. *The Supernatural Tales of Fitz-James O'Brien*. New York: Doubleday, 1988.
————, ed. *Tales By Moonlight II*. New York: Tor, 1989.
————, ed. *What Did Miss Darrington See?* New York: Feminist Press, 1989.
Sarrantonio, Al. *The Boy with the Penny Eyes*. New York: Tor, 1987.
————. *October*. New York: Tor, 1990.
Schow, David J., ed. *Silver Scream*. Arlington Heights: Dark Harvest, 1988.
————. *The Kill Riff*. New York: Tor, 1988.
————. *Lost Angels*. New York: Onyx-NAL, 1990.
————. *Seeing Red*. New York: Tor, 1990.
————. *The Shaft*. London: Macdonald, 1990.
————. *Black Leather Required*. Shingletown Ca.: Mark V. Ziesing, 1994.
Shea, Michael. *Polyphemus*. Sauk City: Arkham House, 1987.
Shepard, Lucius. *The Jaguar Hunter*. Sauk City: Arkham House, 1987.
————. *The Ends of the Earth*. Sauk City: Arkham House, 1991.
————. *The Golden*. Shingletown: Mark V. Ziesing, 1993.
Shiner, Lewis. *Glimpses*. New York: Morrow, 1993.
Shirley, John. *Heatseeker*. Los Angeles: Scream/Press, 1989.
————. *Wetbones*. Shingletown: Mark V. Ziesing, 1991.
Silva, David, ed. *The Definitive Best of the Horror Show*. Baltimore: CD Publications, 1993.
Silva, David, and Paul F. Olsen, eds. *Post Mortem*. New York: St. Martin's Press, 1989. New York: Dell Abyss, 1992.
Simmons, Dan. *Song of Kali*. New York: Bluejay, 1985.
————. *Carrion Comfort*. Arlington Heights: Dark Harvest, 1989.
————. *Prayers to Broken Stones*. Arlington Heights: Dark Harvest, 1990.
————. *Summer of Night*. New York: Putnam, 1991.
————. *Children of the Night*. New York: Putnam, 1992.
————. *Lovedeath*. New York: Warner, 1993.
Skipp, John, and Craig Spector. *Book of the Dead*. New York: Bantam, 1989.
Smith, Clark Ashton. *A Rendezvous in Averoigne*. Sauk City: Arkham House, 1988.

Somtow, S. P. *Vampire Junction*. Norfolk/Virginia Beach: Danning/Starblaze, 1984.

——. *Valentine*. New York: Tor, 1992.

Stableford, Brian. *The Empire of Fear*. London: Simon & Schuster UK, 1988. New York: Carroll & Graf, 1991.

——. *The Werewolves of London*. London: Simon & Schuster UK, 1990. New York: Carrol & Graf, 1992.

——. *Young Blood*. London: Simon & Schuster UK, 1992.

Steakley, John. *Vampire$*. New York: Roc, 1990.

Stoker, Bram. *Dracula*. London: Constable, 1897.

Straub, Peter. *Marriages*. New York: Coward, McCann, & Geoghegan, 1973.

——. *If You Could See Me Now*. New York: Pocket Books, 1976.

——. *Julia*. New York: Pocket Books, 1976.

——. *Ghost Story*. New York: Pocket Books, 1980.

——. *Shadowland*. New York: Berkley, 1981.

——. *Floating Dragon*. New York: G. E. Putnam's Sons, 1982.

——. *The General's Wife*. West Kingston: Donald M. Grant, Inc., 1982.

——. *Leeson Park and Belsize Square*. San Francisco: Underwood-Miller, 1983.

——. *The Blue Rose*. San Francisco: Underwood-Miller, 1985.

——. *Under Venus*. New York: Berkley, 1985.

——. *Koko*. New York: Dutton, 1988.

——. *Houses Without Doors*. New York: Dutton, 1990.

——. *Mrs. God*. Hampton Falls: Donald Grant, 1990.

——. *Mystery*. New York: Dutton, 1990.

——. *The Throat*. New York: Dutton, 1993.

Strieber, Whitley. *The Wolfen*. New York: Morrow, 1978.

——. *The Hunger*. New York: Morrow, 1981.

——. *Black Magic*. New York: Pocket, 1982.

——. *The Night Church*. New York: Simon & Schuster, 1983.

——. *Wolf of Shadows*. New York: Knopf, 1985.

——. *Communion*. New York: Beech Tree-Morrow, 1987.

——. *Transformation*. New York: Beech Tree-Morrow, 1988.

——. *Majestic*. New York: Putnam, 1989.

——. *Billy*. New York: Putnam, 1990.

——. *The Wild*. New York: Tor, 1991.

——. *Unholy Fire*. New York: Dutton, 1992.

——. *The Forbidden Zone*. New York: Dutton, 1993.

Strieber, Whitley, and James W. Kunetka. *Warday: And the Journey Onward*. New York: Holt, Rinehart, and Winston, 1984.

——, and James Kunetka, *Nature's End*. New York: Warner, 1986.

Sullivan, Tim, ed. *Tropical Chills*. New York: Avon, 1988.

Tem, Steve Rasnic. *Excavation*. New York: Avon, 1987.

Tessier, Thomas. *Phantom*. New York: Atheneum, 1982.

Theroux, Paul. *Chicago Loop*. New York: Random House, 1991.

Tryon, Thomas. *The Other*. New York: Knopf, 1971.

———. *The Night of the Moonbow*. New York: Knopf, 1989.

Vachss, Andrew. *Shella*. New York: Knopf, 1993.

Van Buren, Jeanne, and Jack Dann, eds. *In the Field of Fire*. New York: Tor, 1987.

Walpole, Horace. *The Castle of Otranto: A Gothic Story*. London: Tomas Lownds, 1765.

West, Paul. *The Women of Whitechapel and Jack the Ripper*. New York: Random House, 1991.

Whitten, Leslie. *Progeny of the Adder*. New York: Doubleday, 1965.

Wiggins, Marianne. *John Dollar*. New York: Harper & Row, 1989.

Williamson, Chet. *Ash Wednesday*. New York: Tor, 1987.

———. *Lowland Rider*. New York: Tor, 1988.

———. *Dreamthorpe*. Arlington Heights: Dark Harvest, 1989.

Williamson, J. N., ed. *Masques II*. Baltimore: Maclay, 1987.

Wilson, Paul F. *The Keep*. New York: Morrow, 1981.

Winter, Douglas E., ed. *Prime Evil: New Stories by the Masters of Modern Horror*. New York: NAL, 1988.

Wright, T. M. *The Playground*. 1982. New York: Tor, 1982.

Wyndham, John (pseud. of John Benyon Harris). *The Midwich Cuckoos*. London: M. Joseph, 1957.

Yarbro, Chelsea Quinn. *The Saint-Germain Chronicles*. New York: Pocket, 1983.

Secondary Source Materials

Readers can find information about many of these titles as well as a more wide-ranging guide to secondary literature on horror fiction in the chapters "General Reference Books" by Neil Barron and "History and Criticism" and "Author Studies" by Michael A. Morrison in *Horror Literature: A Readers' Guide,* edited by Neil Barron (Garland, 1990). This is the foremost bibliographic guide to the primary and secondary literature of horror fiction, American and otherwise.

Allen, Thomas B. *Possessed: The True Story of an Exorcism*. New York: Doubleday, 1993.

Bannon, Barbara A. Rev. of *The Wolfen*, by Whitley Strieber. *Publishers Weekly* 3 July 1978: 61.

Barron, Neil, ed. *Anatomy of Wonder*. 3rd ed. New York: R. R. Bowker Co., 1987.

———, ed. *Fantasy Literature: A Reader's Guide*. New York: Garland, 1989.

Bayer-Berenbaum, Linda. *The Gothic Imagination: Expansion in Gothic Literature and Art*. Madison: Fairleigh Dickinson, 1982.

Beahm, George. *The Stephen King Story: A Literary Profile.* Kansas City: Andrews & McMeel, 1991.
Benson, Sheila. Rev. of *The Hunger,* dir. by Tony Scott. *Los Angeles Times* 30 Apr. 1983: Calendar 6.
Berry, Michael. "Horror Talks with Peter Straub." *Horror: The News Magazine of the Horror and Dark Fantasy Field.* Jan. 1994: 1, 91–94.
Bettelheim, Bruno. *The Uses of Enchantment: The Meaning and Importance of Fairy Tales.* New York: Knopf, 1976.
Blake, William. *The Portable Blake.* New York: Viking, 1968.
Blatty, William Peter. *William Peter Blatty on The Exorcist from Novel to Film.* New York: Bantam, 1974.
Bleiler, Everett F. *The Guide to Supernatural Fiction.* Kent: Kent State University Press, 1983.
———. *Supernatural Fiction Writers: Fantasy and Horror.* 2 vols. New York: Scribner, 1985.
Bloom, Harold, ed. *Classic Horror Writers.* New York: Chelsea House, 1994.
Bosky, Bernadette. "Stephen King and Peter Straub: Fear and Friendship." *Discovering Stephen King.* Ed. Darrell Schweitzer. Mercer Island: Starmont House, 1985.
———. "Peter Straub: From *Academe* to *Shadowland.*" *Discovering Modern Horror Fiction II.* Ed. Darrell Schweitzer. Mercer Island: Starmont House, 1988.
———. "Theseus in Millhaven," Rev. of *The Throat,* by Peter Straub. *Necrofile: The Review of Horror Fiction* 9 (1993): 4–6.
———. "Haunting and Healing: Memory and Guilt in the Fiction of Peter Straub." *The New York Review of Science Fiction* Sept. 1994: 1, 8–13.
Brigg, Julia. *Night Visitors.* London: Faber, 1977.
Buranelli, Vincent. *Edgar Allan Poe.* 2nd ed. Boston: Twayne, 1977.
Burgess, Michael. *Reference Guide to Science Fiction, Fantasy, and Horror.* Englewood: Libraries Unlimited, 1992.
Büssing, Sabine. *Aliens in the Home: The Child in Horror Fiction.* Westport: Greenwood Press, 1987.
Carlson, Eric W., ed. *Critical Essays on Edgar Allan Poe.* Boston: G. K. Hall, 1987.
Carpenter, Lynette, and Wendy K. Kolmar, eds. *Haunting the House of Fiction: Feminist Perspectives on Ghost Stories by American Women.* Knoxville: University of Tennessee Press, 1991.
Carroll, Noël. *The Philosophy of Horror, or Paradoxes of the Heart.* New York: Routledge, 1990.
Carter, Margaret L. *Spectre or Delusion? The Supernatural in Gothic Fiction.* Ann Arbor: UMI Research Press, 1987.
Casebeer, Edwin F. "The Three Genres of *The Stand.*" *The Dark Descent: Essays Defining Stephen King's Horrorscape.* Ed. Tony Magistrale. Westport, Conn.: Greenwood Press, 1992, 47–59.

———. "Peter Straub's *Shadowland:* The Initiation of a Magician." *The Journal of the Fantastic in the Arts,* 1994.

Clover, Carol. *Men, Women, and Chainsaws: Gender in the Modern Horror Film.* Princeton: Princeton University Press, 1992.

Collins, Robert A., and Robert Latham, eds. *Science Fiction & Fantasy Book Review Annual 1988.* Westport: Meckler, 1988.

———, eds. *Science Fiction & Fantasy Book Review Annual 1989.* Westport: Meckler, 1990.

———, eds. *Science Fiction & Fantasy Book Review Annual 1990.* Westport: Greenwood Press, 1991.

———, eds. *Science Fiction & Fantasy Book Review Annual 1991.* Westport: Greenwood Press, 1994.

Conroy, Ed. *Report on Communion.* New York: Morrow, 1989.

Cox, Greg. *The Transylvanian Library: A Consumer's Guide to Vampire Fiction.* San Bernardino: Borgo Press, 1993.

Daniels, Les. *Living in Fear: A History of Horror in Mass Media.* New York: Scribner, 1975.

"Dark Victory." *The Nation* 20 April 1992: 507–508.

Day, William Patrick. *In the Circles to Fear and Desire: A Study of Gothic Fantasy.* Chicago: University of Chicago Press, 1985.

Dunning, Jennifer. "Behind the Best Sellers: Peter Straub." *New York Times Book Review* 20 May 1979: 56.

Dziemianowicz, Stefan R. *The Annotated Guide to the Unknown and Unknown Worlds.* Mercer Island: Starmont House, 1991.

Edel, Leon, ed. *The Ghostly Tales of Henry James.* New Brunswick: Rutgers University Press, 1948.

Fairchild, Hoxie Neale. *The Romantic Quest.* 1931. New York: Russell & Russell, 1965.

Fiedler, Leslie. *Love and Death in the American Novel.* Rev. ed. New York: Stein & Day, 1966.

Frank, Frederick S. *Through the Pale Door: A Guide to and through the American Gothic.* Westport: Greenwood Press, 1990.

———. *Guide to the Gothic II: An Annotated Bibliography of Criticism.* Metuchen: Scarecrow, 1995.

Gagne, Paul. "An Interview with Peter Straub." *American Fantasy* Feb. 1982: 8–26.

Garrett, Greg. "Objecting to Objectification: Re-Viewing the Feminine in *The Silence of the Lambs.*" *Journal of Popular Culture* 27 (1994): 1–12.

Goldstein, William. "A Coupla Authors Sittin' Around Talkin'." *The Stephen King Companion.* Ed. George Beahm. Kansas City: Andrews and McMeel, 1989.

Gregory, Jay. "TZ Interview: Peter Straub." *Twilight Zone Magazine* May 1981: 1–16.

Grenander, M. E. *Ambrose Bierce.* New York: Twayne, 1971.

Gross, Louis S. *Redefining the American Gothic: From* Wieland *to* Day of the Dead. Ann Arbor: UMI Research Press, 1989.

Heller, Terry. *The Delights of Terror: An Aesthetics of the Tale of Terror.* Urbana: University of Illinois Press, 1987.

Hillman, James. *Revisioning Psychology.* New York: Harper & Row, 1975.

Howells, Coral Ann. *Love, Mystery, and Misery: Feeling in Gothic Fiction.* London: Athlone Press, 1978.

Hyneman, Esther F. *Edgar Allan Poe: Annotated Bibliography of Books and Articles in English, 1827–1973.* Boston: G. K. Hall, 1974.

Jackson, Rosemary. *Fantasy: The Literature of Subversion.* New York: Methuen, 1981.

Johnson, Mary Lynn. "Feminist Approaches to Teaching *Songs.*" *Approaches to Teaching Blake's* Songs of Innocence and of Experience. Eds. Robert F. Glecknew and Mark L. Greenberg. New York: Modern Language Association, 1989.

Jones, Robert K. *The Shudder Pulps: A History of the Weird Menace Magazines of the 1930's.* West Linn: FAX Collector's Edition, 1975. New York: New American Library-Plume, 1978.

Jones, Stephen, and Ramsey Campbell, eds. *Best New Horror.* London: Robinson, 1993.

———— and Kim Newman, eds. *Horror: 100 Best Books.* New York: Carroll & Graf, 1988.

Joshi, S. T. *H. P. Lovecraft: Four Decades of Criticism.* Athens: Ohio University Press, 1980.

————. *H. P. Lovecraft and Lovecraft Criticism: An Annotated Bibliography.* Kent: Kent State University Press, 1981.

————. *H. P. Lovecraft.* Mercer Island: Starmont House, 1982.

————. *The Weird Tale: Arthur Machen, Lord Dunsany, Algernon Blackwood, M. R. James, Ambrose Bierce, H. P. Lovecraft.* Austin: University of Texas Press, 1990.

Jung, Carl G. *The Portable Jung.* Trans. R. F. C. Hull. New York: Viking, 1971.

Kayser, Wolfgang. *The Grotesque in Art and Literature.* Trans. Ulrich Weisstein. Bloomington: Indiana University Press, 1963. New York: Columbia University Press, 1981.

Kazin, Alfred. *The Portable Blake.* New York: Viking, 1968.

Kerr, Howard, John W. Crowley, and Charles W. Crow, eds. *The Haunted Dusk: American Supernatural Fiction, 1820–1920.* Athens: University of Georgia Press, 1983.

King, Stephen. *Danse Macabre.* Rev. ed. New York: Berkley, 1982.

Lasch, Christopher. *Haven in a Heartless World.* New York: Norton, 1977.

————. *The Culture of Narcissism.* New York: Norton, 1979.

Levin, Harry. *The Power of Blackness: Hawthorne, Poe, Melville.* New York: Knopf, 1958.

Lévy, Maurice. *Lovecraft: A Study in the Fantastic.* Trans. S. T. Joshi. Detroit:

Wayne State University Press, 1988. Trans. of *Lovecraft, ou, Du fantastique*. Paris: Christian Bourgois, 1972.

Lopate, Phillip. *The Art of the Personal Essay: An Anthology from the Classical Era to the Present*. New York: Doubleday, 1994.

Lovecraft, Howard Phillips [H. P.]. *Selected Letters*. Vol 1: 1911–1924, ed. by August Derleth and Donald Wandrei. Sauk City: Arkham House, 1965–1976.

———. *Supernatural Horror in Literature*. New York: Ben Abramson, 1945. New York: Dover, 1973.

MacAndrew, Elizabeth. *The Gothic Tradition in Fiction*. New York: Columbia University Press, 1979.

Magistrale, Tony. *Landscape of Fear: Stephen King's American Gothic*. Bowling Green: Bowling Green State University Popular Press, 1988.

———. *The Moral Voyages of Stephen King*. Mercer Island: Starmont House, 1989.

———, ed. The Shining *Reader*. Mercer Island: Starmont House, 1990.

———, ed. *A Casebook on* The Stand. Mercer Island: Starmont House, 1992.

———, ed. *The Dark Descent: Essays Defining Stephen King's Horrorscape*. Westport: Greenwood Press, 1992.

———. *Stephen King: The Second Decade*, Danse Macabre *to* The Dark Half. New York: Twayne, 1992.

Malin, Irving. *New American Gothic*. Carbondale: Southern Illinois University Press, 1962.

McConnel, Frank. *The Spoken Seen: Film and the Romantic Imagination*. Baltimore: Johns Hopkins, 1975.

Munster, Bill, ed. *Sudden Fear: The Horror and Dark Suspense Fiction of Dean R. Koontz*. Mercer Island: Starmont House, 1988.

Neumann, Erich. *The Origins and History of Consciousness*. Trans. R. F. C. Hull. Princeton: Princeton University Press, 1970.

Northey, Margot. *The Haunted Wilderness: The Gothic and Grotesque in Canadian Fiction*. Toronto: University of Toronto Press, 1976.

Paretsky, Sara. "Soft Spot for Serial Murderers." *New York Times* 28 Apr. 1991. Natl. ed.: sec. 4, p. 17.

Parker, Patricia. *Charles Brockden Brown: A Reference Guide*. Boston: G. K. Hall, 1980.

Penzoldt, Peter. *The Supernatural in Fiction*. London: Peter Nevell, 1952.

Pharr, Mary. "Partners in the *Danse:* Women in Stephen King's Fiction." *The Dark Descent: Essays Defining Stephen King's Horrorscape*. Ed. Tony Magistrale. Westport, Conn.: Greenwood Press, 1992.

Praz, Mario. *The Romantic Agony*. New York: Oxford University Press, 1970.

Punter, David. *The Literature of Terror: A History of Gothic Fiction from 1765 to the Present Day*. London: Longman, 1980.

Radcliffe, Elsa J. *Gothic Novels of the Twentieth Century: An Annotated Bibliography*. Metuchen: Scarecrow Press, 1977.

Reagan, Robert. *Poe: A Collection of Critical Essays*. Englewood Cliffs: Prentice-Hall, 1967.

Remise, Jac. *Diableries: La vie quotidienne chez Satan a la fin du 19e siecle.* Poitiers/ Aubin: Ballard, 1978.

Ringe, Donald A. *American Gothic: Imagination and Reason in Nineteenth-Century Fiction.* Lexington: University Press of Kentucky, 1982.

Rogers-Gardner, Barbara. *Jung and Shakespeare.* Wilmette: Chiron Publications, 1992.

Rottensteiner, Franz. *The Fantasy Book: An Illustrated History from Dracula to Tolkien.* London: Thames & Hudson; New York: Macmillan, 1978.

Saliba, David R. *A Psychology of Fear: The Nightmare Formula of Edgar Allan Poe.* Lantham: University Press of America, 1980.

Senf, Carol A. *The Vampire in Nineteenth-Century English Literature.* Bowling Green: Bowling Green State University Popular Press, 1988.

Sheehy, Gail. *Passages.* New York: Dutton, 1976.

Sidney-Fryer, Donald. *Emperor of Dreams: A Clark Ashton Smith Bibliography.* West Kingston: Donald M. Grant, 1978.

Skal, David J. *The Monster Show: A Cultural History of Horror.* New York: Norton & Co., 1993.

Smith, Curtis C., ed. *Twentieth-Century Science-Fiction Writers.* 2nd ed. London: St. James Press, 1981.

Steinberg, Sybil. Rev. of *Billy*, by Whitley Strieber. *Publishers Weekly* 15 June 1990: 56.

Sullivan, Jack, ed. *The Penguin Encyclopedia of Horror and the Supernatural.* New York: Viking, 1986.

Terrell, Carroll F. *Stephen King: Man and Artist.* Rev. ed. Orono: Northern Lights Press, 1991.

Thompson, Gary Richard, ed. *The Gothic Imagination: Essays in Dark Romanticism.* Pullman: Washington State University Press, 1974.

Todorov, Tzvetan. *The Fantastic: A Structural Approach to a Literary Genre.* Trans. Richard Howard. Ithaca: Cornell University Press, 1975. Trans. of *Introductions à Littérature Fantastique.* Paris: Seuil, 1970.

Tropp, Martin. *Images of Fear: How Horror Stories Helped Shape Modern Culture (1818–1918).* Jefferson: McFarland & Co., 1990.

Twitchell, James. *Dreadful Pleasures: An Anatomy of Modern Horror.* New York: Oxford University Press, 1985.

———. *The Living Dead: A Study of the Vampire in Romantic Literature.* Durham: Duke University Press, 1981.

———. *Preposterous Violence: Fables of Aggression in Modern Culture.* New York: Oxford University Press, 1989.

Tymn, Marshall B., ed. *Horror Literature: A Core Collection and Reference Guide.* New York: R. R. Bowker Co., 1981.

——— and Mike Ashley, eds. *Science Fiction, Fantasy, and Weird Fiction Magazines.* Westport: Greenwood Press, 1985.

Varnado, S. L. *Haunted Presence: The Numinous in Gothic Fiction.* Birmingham: University of Alabama Press, 1987.

Wagenknecht, Edward. *Edgar Allan Poe: The Man Behind the Legend.* New York: Oxford University Press, 1963.

Waller, Gregory A. *The Living and the Undead: From Stoker's* Dracula *to Romero's* Dawn of the Dead. Urbana: University of Illinois Press, 1986.

Weinberg, Robert. *The Weird Tales Story.* West Linn: FAX Collector's Edition, 1977.

Wiater, Stanley. "Beyond *Communion:* A Conversation With Whitley Strieber." *Twilight Zone Magazine* Apr. 1988: 22–25.

———. Dark Visions: *Conversations with the Masters of the Horror Film.* New York: Avon, 1992.

Winter, Douglas E. *Stephen King: The Art of Darkness.* New York: NAL, 1984; Plume (expanded and updated), 1986.

———. "Stephen King, Peter Straub, and the Quest for *The Talisman.*" *Twilight Zone Magazine* Jan.–Feb. 1985: 62–65.

———. "Whitley Strieber." *Faces of Fear.* New York: Berkley, 1985. Rev. ed. London: Pan, 1990.

Wood, Robin. *Hollywood from Vietnam to Reagan.* New York: Columbia University Press, 1986.

About the Editors and Contributors

Bernadette Lynn Bosky lives and works in New York City. She is the author of articles about Peter Straub and Stephen King that have appeared in *Discovering Horror Fiction, Kingdom of Fear,* and *The Dark Descent: Essays Defining Stephen King's Horrorscape.* A longtime scholar of the fantastic, she has also published on other writers in the genre, particularly Charles Williams, and on the development of academic criticism of the genre.

Edwin F. Casebeer is a professor of English at Indiana University where he teaches courses in Shakespeare, popular culture, and American studies. He is the author of several published essays on Stephen King, most recently in *The Dark Descent: Essays Defining Stephen King's Horrorscape* and *A Casebook on* The Stand.

Michael J. Collins, a regular contributor to *Necrofile: The Review of Horror Fiction,* is currently at work on a book-length study of the link between violent and subversive strains in contemporary American culture. He lives in New Hampshire with his wife and son.

Lynda Haas is an assistant professor in the writing program at Ithaca College. She is the co-editor of *From Mouse to Mermaid: The Politics of Film, Gender, and Culture,* and has published articles in several journals, including *Teaching English in the Two-Year College* and *PreText.*

Robert Haas teaches film and literature courses at the University of South Florida. He is currently co-editing a book on the supernatural in Victorian literature. He recently contributed an essay on *Billy Bathgate* for the collection *From Mouse to Mermaid,* and guest edited an issue of the journal *PostScript* dedicated to the films of David Cronenberg.

Tony Magistrale has written and edited several books on Stephen King and the American Gothic. He is an associate professor of English at the University of Vermont where he teaches courses on Anglo-American Gothicism and American literature. His most recent book is the Twayne U.S. Authors volume on Stephen King.

Michael A. Morrison holds a joint professorship in the departments of English and Physics at the University of Oklahoma. He is the author of many articles, reviews, and bibliographic criticism in the fields of fantasy, science fiction, and horror. He is currently writing a book on the roles of science and the scientist in contemporary culture.

Mary Pharr is an accomplished scholar on film and in studies on the fantastic. Her essays on Stephen King have appeared in several collections including *The Gothic World of Stephen King, A Casebook on* The Stand and *The Dark Descent: Essays Defining Stephen King's Horrorscape.* She teaches in the English department at Florida Southern College.

Douglas E. Winter is an attorney who lives in Washington, D.C. He has written and published both horror fiction and criticism. He is the author of the critical biography *Stephen King: The Art of Darkness,* the interviewer and compiler of *Faces of Fear: Encounters with the Creators of Modern Horror,* and the editor of *Prime Evil: New Stories by the Masters of Modern Horror.*

Index

Ackroyd, Peter, 17
adaptations: film, 90–91, 95–96, 103, 113, 117–19
alien visitors, 103–4
anthologies, 18
archetypes: horror genre, 21–25, 27–28, 99
automata, 111–12

Barker, Clive, 46–47, 120–21
best-sellers, 11–13
Bettelheim, Bruno, 74
Blake, William, 28–31, 36
Blatty, William Peter: association with comic books, 85; *Exorcist, The,* 9, 84, 86–91, 93–94, (film) 115–17; *Exorcist II: The Heretic* (film), 91; *Exorcist III* (film), 95; Hollywood involvement, 86; *Legion,* 92–95; *Ninth Configuration, The,* 92–93
body: emphasis on in horror fiction, 65, 67n33
Brown, Charles Brockden, 1
Butler, Jack, 17

cannibalism, 33
Carroll, Noël, 4, 7, 39
cave art, 110
characterization: methods of, 45–47, 75–78
cinematic techniques in horror art, 113–14, 117, 121
Clover, Carol, 6, 118
Conroy, Ed, 103
consciousness: states of, 78–79
Corman, Roger, 113

dark suspense, 23
death, 44, 98
detective fiction: link to horror, 33–35, 69, 88
Dika, Vera, 118
Dionysian vs. Apollonian forces, 39, 61
Dracula, 47, 57, 65, 121

Etchison, Dennis, 25–26

fairy tales, 74–75
family: in horror genre, 48–50, 76–77
feminism: Gothic sexuality, 31–38, 65
Fiedler, Leslie, 1–2, 26
Frankenstein, 7, 62, 113

Garrett, Greg, 38
gender hybrids: in horror, 16–18, 33–35, 43, 69–70, 73–76, 81, 88, 111
good and evil, 91–95
Gothic: American, 1–2, 25–26, 98
Gothic: British, 1, 31, 56–57, 62, 66n3, 111
Gothic heroines, 5–6, 29, 34–38, 53–54, 80
Gothic (horror) novels: contemporary, 2, 6, 11–26, 62, 76; eighteenth century, 1, 4–5, 11, 22, 31, 33, 57, 62, 66n3, 111; New England, 48; nineteenth century, 14, 98, 110–12
Gothic: narrative modes, 31
Grant, Charles L., 18

Harris, Thomas, 24; *Black Sunday,* 28, 33–34; monsters in his fiction, 33–